Sweet things

Sweet things

An irresistible collection of sweet, not too sweet and sweet and savoury dishes

SUZANNE GIBBS

Angus&Robertson

An imprint of HarperCollins*Publishers*

Page one: Rose-water flavours the cordial (page 75) for this wonderfully refreshing drink which looks a picture when finished with pomegranate seeds.

Page two: Strawberry Galette Tarts (page 89). Strawberries, raspberries and cream make a fabulous dessert sandwiched with almond and hazelnut meringue hearts.

An Angus & Robertson Publication

Angus&Robertson, an imprint of
HarperCollins*Publishers*
25 Ryde Road, Pymble, Sydney, NSW 2073, Australia
31 View Road, Glenfield, Auckland 10, New Zealand

First published in Australia in 1994

National Library of Australia
Cataloguing-in-Publication data:

Gibbs, Suzanne.
    Sweet things.
    Includes index.
    ISBN 0 207 18241 8
    1. Cookery (Sugar). 2. Cookery (fruit). 3. Confectionery.
    4. Desserts. I. Title.
641.86

A BARBARA BECKETT BOOK

Produced in association with
Barbara Beckett Publishing
14 Hargrave Street, Paddington, Sydney, Australia 2021

Food by Suzanne Gibbs and Margaret Fulton
Photography by Rodney Weidland
Jacket design by Melanie Feddersen
Printed in Hong Kong

CONTENTS

Above: Fresh seasonal fruits are the very best of sweet things. Almost any combination of fruit can begin or end a meal on a high note.

Left: Cooking is a pleasure when the right equipment is at hand. A fine collection such as this can be built up over a few years of visiting specialist cookery shops.

Foreword

Suzanne Gibbs is the perfect author for a book entitled *Sweet Things*. An extraordinarily good cook, complete with the prestigious London Cordon Bleu Diploma and the experience of a year spent in charge of the pastry and dessert kitchen of the Cordon Bleu Restaurant in Marylebone Lane, Suzanne knows a lot about sweet things. Not only cakes, puddings, desserts and sweetmeats, but also savouries, salads, poultry, meats and vegetarian dishes benefit from Suzanne's delicate 'sweet touch'. An inspiration and a lovely book. A must for sweet tooths and those who enjoy good food.

Margaret Fulton

Margaret Fulton

Weights and Measures

...ipes in this book are given in metric ...easures, using standard measuring cups and spoons. In brackets are the imperial equivalents. These translations are not exact equivalents but brought to the nearest round figure; however, they will preserve the correct balance of ingredients. To retain that balance, follow either metric or imperial, never a mixture.

All Good Cooks Need

• A nest of four graduated measuring cups for measuring dry ingredients. These come in ¼, ½, ⅓ and 1-cup size.

• A standard measuring cup for measuring liquids.
• A 1-litre, 4-cup or 1-pint measuring jug for measuring liquids.
These jugs usually show both cup and metric measures and are marked in cups and millilitres, others in imperial fluid ounces.
• A set of graduated measuring spoons.
The set includes a tablespoon, teaspoon, half-teaspoon and quarter-teaspoon. Level spoon measures are used.
• Scales. Usually marked nowadays in both metric and imperial measurements. Scales are needed for weighing meat, vegetables and bulky items.

Spoon and Cup Measurements

	Australia	New Zealand	United Kingdom	United States
1 tablespoon	20 ml	15 ml	½ fl oz (14 ml)	½ fl oz (15 ml)
1 cup	250 ml	250 ml	8 fl oz (227 ml)	8 fl oz (237 ml)

All countries use the same teaspoon measurements.

Preheat the Oven

Always preheat an oven, unless you are reheating food. The time this takes varies with the oven. As so many cookery procedures vary, like chilling pastry for an hour or folding in egg whites for a soufflé in 3 minutes, it is not practical to include instructions to preheat the oven at the beginning of each recipe. Keep this in mind when using the oven and make sure it is at the required temperature by the time you are ready to put the dish in the oven.

The usual time to reach a required oven temperature varies from 15 to 20 minutes. Check with the instruction book of your oven.

The correct oven temperature is essential to the success of a dish. It makes pastry crisp, a soufflé or cake rise. Only a high heat will seal in meat juices—too low a heat draws the juices out. Sometimes oven temperatures are changed during cooking, high heat for a crispy topping, then low to cook the filling.

Acknowledgments

No cookbook author could be better off than I in having Margaret Fulton, the doyenne of Australian food writers, as a mother. She has inspired me with her love of food and cooking all my life. In my own career as a food writer, she has constantly encouraged without ever being assertive. During the writing of *Sweet Things*, she was the one person from whom I would seek advice with absolute confidence.

I would like to thank Barbara Beckett for her faith in my work in suggesting that I would be just the person for a book entitled *Sweet Things*. She has always been a pleasure to work with and her professionalism as a publisher is strongly reflected in the book.

Working with Rodney Weidland as photographer has been a joy. He embraces his subject with such care and thought that it was a true inspiration to be working alongside him. He had confidence in my food, and captured in his photographs the true shapes, colours and textures of each dish.

I would also like to thank Amber Keller and Iris Silva, who assisted me in the kitchen. Together they made the book possible with all their shopping, chopping, listening and watching, so that every task was completed without there ever being any sign of chaos.

Suzanne Gibbs

Suzanne Gibbs

INTRODUCTION

Every day we use words that identify sweetness with love and pleasure. Words like 'sweetheart', 'honey' and 'sugar' are common terms of endearment. In the Old Testament, the promised land is described as a land flowing with milk and honey, a metaphor of delightful plenty.

A book on sweet things is a book about some of the most pleasurable things in life.

Along with recipes for pastries, cakes and confectionery, my book includes ways of cooking sweet baby peas, young carrots, fragrant fruits, those things that, when at their best, happen to be also at their sweetest.

With even a quick flip through the pages you will discover that the term 'sweet things' doesn't necessarily imply sugar-laden. A piece of perfect fruit is as prized as the most elaborate and exotic sweet dish. What, for instance, could be more delicious than perfect sweet berries and thick cream? The natural sugars and tartness of the fruit provide the perfect balance with the cream. When fruit is at its best, nothing else is needed.

On the other hand, to set aside a few hours in which to enjoy cooking something more elaborate, like baking a cake, with all the care it deserves, is wonderfully rewarding, even therapeutic, especially when it is received with tones of glee at the table and every mouthful relished with true appreciation.

Of the four basic taste sensations—sweet, sour, salty and bitter—sweetness is the only one for which we have an innate liking. This is probably a relic of the fruit-eating habits of our distant ancestors. Apart from an inborn dislike for bitterness, our taste is moulded by social custom, opportunity and associations with pleasurable or painful moments.

Ultimately it is the combining of these taste sensations that makes cooking the art it is today, and makes eating one of our greatest pleasures. There's a fascination in mixing sweet and sour, sharp and sweet, sweet and spicy—the combinations are limitless.

The tartness of lemon and the sweetness of sugar are just what a pancake needs. Tart and sweet raspberries blended with sugar and vinegar make a raspberry vinegar that transforms salads and drinks. Naturally sweet baby onions and currants take on a new dimension when cooked with a sharp wine vinegar. Duck with cherries or orange is well known and a favourite with many, but the possibilities don't end there; duck with fresh grapes is a beautiful autumn dish.

King Charles I liked orange jellies served as wedges in the orange skin as a refresher before he tackled a more serious dish. So do I. For the ultimate sweet and fragrant combination, delicate Turkish delight calls for lemon, rose-water and pistachios.

Sweet Things embraces the practical and the fantastic, the seasonal and the exotic, foods that we can enjoy every day and those that are and should remain a rare treat.

In selecting recipes for this book, I have focused on the best of all these qualities, a task that has been a great joy.

The Special Equipment

With the growth of specialist cookery shops, those of us who like to cook and bake are gradually stocking our kitchens with the things that make cooking such a pleasure, things like madeleine moulds for making those divine shell-like cakes so beloved of the French, and the various kinds of pastry moulds and other devices. Those special things may be expensive, but over the years you can build up your collection.

Here is a random list of some of the specialty equipment from my own kitchen, those things that I find invaluable in making the tarts, pies, pastries and sweetmeats that have been included in this book.

Measuring cups, spoons, jugs in standard measuring sizes. Scales for heavy items such as meats, fish and poultry.

A good, solid pastry board and several chopping boards. A marble slab for pastry and confectionery is a bonus; look for one in second-hand shops.

Baking trays (sheets) for biscuits and cookies,

Overleaf: An offering of delectable fruit tartlets, melt-in-the-mouth meringues and a superb rich walnut tart makes the ultimate afternoon tea.

scones, tarts and so on: one or two black metal, one or two aluminium.

Silicone (parchment) paper for baking. It can be used many times; no ingredient will stick to it and it is a great plus.

Wire cooling racks, round and square.

Round flan tins (pie pans) of different sizes for pastries, tarts and cakes such as Linzertorte (page 26). You may also select square or oblong shapes.

Fluted quiche rings with removable bases: 20 cm (8 in), 23 cm (9 in) and 25 cm (10 in) are good sizes.

Springform pans for cheesecakes, delicate and Continental cakes.

Trays for small and large madeleines, shell-shaped.

Plain round, fluted and boat-shaped tartlet pans.

An assortment of pastry cutters, in sets or individual: round, square, heart, diamond, plain, fluted and novelty shapes.

A wooden rolling pin for pastry.

Small firm sharp knives and palette knives; also a flexible palette knife.

Aluminium baking beans for baking blind (page 160). They are heavier than dried beans, which can be too light.

Rectangular straight-sided cake pans for bar cakes, loaves and the like. Aim for two different sizes.

Pairs of 20 cm (8 in), 23 cm (9 in) or 25 cm (10 in) cake pans, straight-sided. Also invest in the slightly sloping moule manque pans favoured for gâteaux.

Muffin pans, large and small, also patty pans for small cakes and tartlets.

An assortment of pastry brushes, and wooden, metal and rubber spatulas.

A flour or sugar dredger.

Piping (pastry) bags and nozzles in various sizes. Light bags are used for meringues and the like, heavier ones for heavier mixtures.

A plastic scraper for cleaning out bowls, a plastic serrated comb for mixing chocolate or decorating biscuits such as Florentines (page 48).

A sugar thermometer—inexpensive and useful.

An electric mixer for cakes, batters and so on. A hand rotary beater for light mixtures; buy a good, strong one with smooth action and wire whisks for sauces and creams. A food processor is no longer considered a luxury; it has multiple uses.

Tools for coring apples, cutting strips of zest from citrus fruits, producing round melon balls, curling butter—and more.

Get a picture of the pieces of equipment you will use. Some you will use again and again; others you will reserve for special occasions. Add slowly to your basic collection after considering whether an item will really earn its keep and storage space in your kitchen.

A word about care of your collection. Wash metal cake pans, trays, piping nozzles, and the like, in sudsy water, remove any burnt bits, rinse and dry well. Pop them into a cooling oven to dry properly. Store in a dry place to avoid rust. Egg beaters, whisks and pastry brushes must always be scrupulously clean and dry.

Don't allow a novice to use your very special equipment for jobs other than that for which it was designed; for example, cracking nuts with a rolling pin, getting the top off a bottle or cutting a hose pipe with a good knife. Like any good tradesman, treat your tools of trade with the greatest respect.

I have inherited some of my grandmother's kitchen treasures. They have done valiant service in three generations of kitchens, and that is how it should be.

CAKES

Cakemaking always seems to have played an important part in our kitchens, our lives, history, celebrations, and even our language—'it's a piece of cake' says a lot.

The French celebrate success with gâteau progrès. A German housewife makes two stollens at Christmas —one to give and one to keep. Anne Boleyn enjoyed maids of honour, the small almond-filled tarts collected for her by her maids of honour while she waited upon the command of Henry VIII. In Australia's outback, powder puffs languished in an airtight container waiting for the vicar to call.

Celebrating with a cake is indeed a very old custom, as old perhaps as the joy derived from baking a beautiful cake in one's own oven.

Almond Sherry Cake

A lovely simple butter and almond cake, especially good with a glass of sherry or other wine.

250 G (8 OZ) BUTTER

1 CUP (7 OZ) CASTER (SUPERFINE) SUGAR

2 TABLESPOONS SHERRY (USE THE SHERRY YOU LIKE TO DRINK)

4 MEDIUM EGGS

1¼ CUPS (4 OZ) GROUND ALMONDS

2½ CUPS (10 OZ) PLAIN (ALL-PURPOSE) FLOUR

1 TEASPOON BAKING POWDER

½ TEASPOON SALT

Preheat the oven to 160°C (325°F). Grease and line a deep 20 cm (8 in) cake pan with baking paper (parchment).

Cream the butter and gradually add the sugar, beating until the batter is light and fluffy. Beat in the sherry. Add the eggs, one at a time, beating well after each addition. Sprinkle in a little flour if the batter looks like curdling.

Stir in the ground almonds. Sift the flour with the baking powder and salt, and fold this into the creamed batter. Turn it into a cake pan. Bake in the centre of the oven for 45 minutes, then reduce the heat to (150°C/300°F), and bake for a further 30–45 minutes, until a skewer inserted comes out clean. Leave to stand for a few minutes before turning out to cool on a wire rack.

SERVES 6–8

Lemon Tea Cake

Make this in a loaf pan or ring pan. As soon as the cake comes out of the oven, sprinkle it with lemon juice to give it a lovely sharp fresh-tasting tang.

1½ CUPS (6 OZ) PLAIN (ALL-PURPOSE) FLOUR

1 CUP (8 OZ) SUGAR

1½ TEASPOONS BAKING POWDER

A PINCH OF SALT

125 G (4 OZ) BUTTER

2 LARGE EGGS, BEATEN

½ CUP (4 FL OZ) MILK

GRATED RIND OF 1 LEMON

½ CUP (2 OZ) CHOPPED PECANS OR WALNUTS

JUICE OF 1 LEMON

3 TABLESPOONS SUGAR

Preheat the oven to 180°C (350°F). Grease a 23 x 13 x 8 cm (9 x 5 x 3 in) loaf pan or 20 cm (8 in) ring (tube) pan. Line the bottom with baking paper (parchment).

Sift the flour, sugar, baking powder and salt together into a bowl. Rub in the butter with your fingertips until the mixture resembles breadcrumbs. Mix the eggs and milk together and fold them into the mixture with the grated rind and nuts. Pour the batter into the prepared pan and bake until the cake is firm to the touch and a skewer inserted comes out clean—about 1 hour and 20 minutes for a loaf pan, 50 minutes for a ring.

Mix the lemon juice and sugar together and, when the cake is cooked, sprinkle it over the top. Leave the cake to cool in the pan before turning it out.

SERVES 8

Overleaf: Clockwise from left: Gâteau Progrès, a celebration cake made with layers of nut meringue and coffee butter cream; Vacherin, a meringue cake, this one filled with chestnut cream and topped with glacé chestnuts; and a Linzertorte, the famous Austrian pastry cake.

Gingerbread

This is how gingerbread cake is meant to be—dark, moist and spicy. Lemon Butter Icing is perfect for it.

1½ CUPS (6 OZ) PLAIN (ALL-PURPOSE) FLOUR
½ TEASPOON BICARBONATE OF SODA (BAKING SODA)
1 TABLESPOON GROUND GINGER
1 TEASPOON GROUND CINNAMON
¼ TEASPOON EACH GROUND CLOVES AND ALLSPICE
125 G (4 OZ) UNSALTED BUTTER
½ CUP (3 OZ) (LIGHT) BROWN SUGAR
½ CUP (4 FL OZ) DE-BITTERED MOLASSES
2 LARGE EGGS
2 TEASPOONS VANILLA ESSENCE (EXTRACT)
½ CUP (4 FL OZ) BUTTERMILK
LEMON BUTTER ICING (PAGE 168) (OPTIONAL)

Preheat the oven to 180°C (350°F). Butter and line a 23 cm (9 in) round cake pan to about 4 cm (1½ in) deep.

Sift the flour, bicarbonate of soda and spices into a bowl. Cream the butter in the bowl of an electric mixer and beat in the brown sugar until the mixture is light and fluffy. Beat the molasses into the butter mixture, then the eggs, one at a time. Lastly beat in the vanilla essence. Stir in the sifted flour mixture thoroughly, then the buttermilk.

Turn the batter into the prepared cake pan, smoothing the top and making a slight indentation in the centre with a spatula. Bake for 35–40 minutes, or until an inserted skewer comes out clean. Let the gingerbread cool in the pan on a wire rack. Turn out onto a serving plate and serve the gingerbread plain or spread with Lemon Butter Icing.

SERVES 8–10

Marion's Banana Cake

My mother-in-law takes after her aunts, who were champion pastrycooks and ran their own successful bakery in New Zealand many years ago. This is one of her specials, a homely banana cake which is a hit with all ages at family gatherings.

125 G (4 OZ) UNSALTED BUTTER
½ CUP (4 OZ) CASTER (SUPERFINE) SUGAR
2 EGGS
2 BANANAS, MASHED SMOOTH
1 TEASPOON BICARBONATE OF SODA (BAKING SODA)
    DISSOLVED IN 2 TABLESPOONS BOILING MILK
2 CUPS (8 OZ) PLAIN (ALL-PURPOSE) FLOUR
1 TEASPOON GROUND CINNAMON (OPTIONAL)
1 TEASPOON BAKING POWDER
1 CUP (8 FL OZ) CREAM, WHIPPED
1 BANANA, SLICED AT THE LAST MOMENT
ICING (CONFECTIONERS') SUGAR, FOR DUSTING

Preheat the oven to 180°C (350°F) and grease and line two 23 cm (9 in) sandwich tins (shallow round cake pans).

Cream the butter and beat in the sugar until the mixture is light and fluffy. Beat in the eggs one at a time, then stir in the mashed banana and the bicarbonate of soda and milk. Sift the flour, cinnamon (if used) and baking powder together and fold into the mixture. Turn the batter into the prepared tins and bake for 20 minutes.

Turn out and cool on wire racks. Fill with whipped cream and sliced bananas. Dust with icing sugar and serve cut into wedges.

SERVES 8–10

Eggs at room temperature will whip to a greater volume than very cold eggs taken straight from the refrigerator.

Savoy Cake

This classic French cake is a light-as-air sponge cake which relies on the beaten egg whites for its height.

1 CUP (8 OZ) CASTER (SUPERFINE) SUGAR
7 EGGS, SEPARATED
2 TEASPOONS VANILLA ESSENCE (EXTRACT)
½ CUP (2 OZ) PLAIN (ALL-PURPOSE) FLOUR
¾ CUP (4 OZ) POTATO FLOUR
ICING (CONFECTIONERS') SUGAR, FOR DUSTING

Preheat the oven to 160°C (325°F). Butter and flour a 25 cm (10 in) round cake pan.

Using an electric mixer, beat the sugar, egg yolks and vanilla at high speed until the mixture is pale and tripled in bulk. Sift the plain and potato flours and fold in gently. In a separate bowl, beat the egg whites until stiff but not dry. Stir a spoonful into the batter, then fold the rest in quickly and lightly.

Turn the batter into the prepared pan. Bake for 1 hour or a little longer until the cake is light golden and a skewer inserted comes out clean. Turn off the oven and leave the cake to rest in the oven with the door open for 10 minutes.

The cake may be eaten as it is. Alternatively, it can be split and filled either with whipped cream sweetened and flavoured with vanilla, or Crème Patissière (page 165). Dust with icing sugar before serving.

SERVES 8–10

Left: French Savoy Cake, made light as air by using potato flour and beaten egg whites. Below: Four-Quarter Cake with plums.

Four-Quarter Cake

Four-quarter cake is a time-honoured recipe which traditionally calls for measuring out the sugar, butter and flour so that each equals the weight of the eggs. This version is not so rich.

4 LARGE EGGS, SEPARATED
1½ CUPS (12 OZ) CASTER (SUPERFINE) SUGAR
1 TABLESPOON GRATED LEMON RIND OR
   1 TEASPOON VANILLA ESSENCE (EXTRACT)
375 G (12 OZ) UNSALTED BUTTER, SOFTENED
3 CUPS (12 OZ) PLAIN (ALL-PURPOSE) FLOUR,
   SIFTED WITH ½ TEASPOON SALT
8–10 FRESH PLUMS, HALVED AND PITTED,
   OR 1 CUP (6 OZ) PITTED PRUNES
ICING (CONFECTIONERS') SUGAR, SIFTED, FOR
   DUSTING

Preheat the oven to 180°C (350°F). Butter and flour a 28 x 20 cm (11 x 8 in) cake pan.

Using a whisk and a bowl over a pan of hot water, or an electric mixer, beat the yolks and sugar with the flavouring until very thick and lemon-coloured. Beat in the soft butter gradually, and finally fold in the sifted flour. Lastly whisk the egg whites separately, and fold them quickly and lightly into the cake batter, using a large metal spoon. Turn the batter into the pan. Top with the fruit and bake for 35–40 minutes or until firm to the touch.

Turn out onto a wire rack, invert fruit-side up, and dust with sifted icing sugar. Leave to cool or serve warm with whipped cream or ice cream.

SERVES 8

Orange Flower Honey Cake

A delicate cake which doesn't rise as high as the more common sponge cakes, but does have a lovely moistness and flavour. From Spain, it is traditionally made from 'miel de azahar', honey from the orange flower.

¾ CUP (6 FL OZ) HONEY (PREFERABLY ORANGE FLOWER)

2 EGGS, SEPARATED

3 TABLESPOONS CASTER (SUPERFINE) SUGAR

1 TEASPOON ORANGE FLOWER WATER

1 TEASPOON OLIVE OIL

½ CUP (2 OZ) PLAIN (ALL-PURPOSE) FLOUR

½ TEASPOON DRIED (ACTIVE DRY) YEAST

¼ TEASPOON GROUND CINNAMON

ICING (CONFECTIONERS') SUGAR, FOR DUSTING

Preheat the oven to 200°C (400°F). Brush a 20 cm (8 in) round cake pan with olive oil and dust with flour.

Heat the honey gently over a saucepan of hot water until it turns liquid. Meanwhile, beat the egg yolks with the sugar until thick and pale. Add the warm honey, orange flower water and oil, stirring. Sift the flour with the yeast and ground cinnamon, and add it gradually to the mixture, folding gently.

Whisk the egg whites until soft peaks form and carefully fold into the cake batter. Turn the batter into the prepared pan. Bake for 30–40 minutes until firm and golden. Cool a few minutes in the pan, then turn out and cool on a wire rack. Dust the top with sifted icing sugar.

SERVES 6

Caster (superfine) sugar dissolves more readily than ordinary white crystal sugar and will give a sponge a fine, light texture.

Glazed Sour Cream Apple Cake

A very pretty cake which can be served warm or at room temperature with softly whipped cream.

2 GOLDEN DELICIOUS APPLES

JUICE OF 1 LEMON

185 G (6 OZ) BUTTER

1 CUP (7 OZ) CASTER (SUPERFINE) SUGAR

3 LARGE EGGS

½ TEASPOON VANILLA ESSENCE (EXTRACT)

1⅓ CUPS (5½ OZ) SELF-RAISING (SELF-RISING) FLOUR, SIFTED

4 TABLESPOONS GROUND ALMONDS

2 TABLESPOONS (DAIRY) SOUR CREAM

3 TABLESPOONS APRICOT JAM

Preheat the oven to 190°C (375°F). Butter a 20 cm (8 in) springform pan.

Peel the apples, cut them into quarters and cut away the cores. Slice the apple quarters thinly, not quite through to the core side, and place them in a bowl of water with the lemon juice.

Cream the butter and beat in the sugar gradually until light and fluffy. Beat in the eggs one at a time, then beat in the vanilla essence. Fold in the flour with the almonds and sour cream until well mixed. Spoon the batter into the buttered springform pan.

Arrange the drained apple quarters decoratively over the cake batter and bake in the middle of the oven for 40 minutes or until a skewer inserted comes out clean.

Meanwhile, melt the jam in a small saucepan. Rub the melted jam through a sieve and use it to brush over the cake as soon as it is taken from the oven. Leave the cake to cool in the pan for about 10 minutes. Run a small spatula around the edge of the cake to loosen it, then remove the springform sides.

SERVES 6–8

Sachertorte

This is Vienna's most famous cake, elegantly simple and really luscious. It is a rich chocolate sponge spread with apricot jam and given a thin coating of special chocolate icing. It has become fashionable to serve whipped cream with Sachertorte, though many prefer it without.

200 G (6½ OZ) DARK (SEMI-SWEET) COOKING
   CHOCOLATE
125 G (4 OZ) UNSALTED BUTTER
1 TEASPOON VANILLA ESSENCE (EXTRACT)
8 EGG YOLKS
10 EGG WHITES
A PINCH OF SALT
¾ CUP (6 OZ) CASTER (SUPERFINE) SUGAR
1 CUP (4 OZ) PLAIN (ALL-PURPOSE) FLOUR
¾ CUP (6FL OZ) APRICOT JAM
GLAZE
125 G (4 OZ) DARK (SEMI-SWEET) COOKING
   CHOCOLATE
1 CUP (8 FL OZ) (LIGHT WHIPPING) CREAM
1 CUP (8 OZ) SUGAR
1 TEASPOON GOLDEN SYRUP (LIGHT TREACLE)
1 EGG WHITE
1 TEASPOON VANILLA ESSENCE (EXTRACT)

Preheat the oven to 180°C (350°F). Grease and line two 23 cm (9 in) sandwich tins (shallow round cake pans) with circles of greased baking paper (parchment).

Melt the chocolate and butter in a bowl over hot water, stirring occasionally with a wooden spoon. Add the vanilla, cool slightly, and beat in the egg yolks one at a time.

In an electric mixer, beat the egg whites slowly with the pinch of salt until frothy, then increase speed and beat until soft peaks form. Add the sugar, 1 tablespoon at a time, and continue beating until thick and glossy. Stir 3 tablespoons of this meringue into the chocolate mixture—this makes it easier to combine the chocolate mixture and the rest of the meringue.

Sift the flour over the chocolate mixture. Using a metal spoon or rubber spatula with an 'over and under' cutting motion, fold together the remaining meringue, chocolate mixture and flour. Do not overmix.

Pour the batter into the prepared tins and bake for 25–30 minutes or until a fine skewer comes out clean when inserted in the centre of the cakes.

Remove the pans from the oven and stand them on wire racks for 20 minutes, then run a knife around the cakes and turn them out. When completely cold, store in sealed containers for 24 hours.

Sieve the jam into a small saucepan, add 1 tablespoon of hot water and heat slightly. Join the cakes with 4 tablespoons of the jam and brush the top and sides with the rest of it.

Glaze. Combine the chocolate, cream, sugar and golden syrup in a small, heavy saucepan. Heat gently until the sugar dissolves, stirring with a wooden spoon, then boil without stirring for 5 minutes. Lightly beat the egg white in a small bowl, then pour in the hot chocolate mixture, beating constantly. Pour the mixture back into the saucepan and cook, stirring, over a gentle heat for 3 minutes. Stir in the vanilla.

Allow the glaze to stand for only a minute. Place the cake on a rack over a baking tray (sheet) and pour the glaze over the cake. When the glaze stops dripping and starts to set, move the cake to a serving dish. Refrigerate until the glaze has hardened.

A Sachertorte can be stored in the refrigerator for several days.

SERVES 8–10

If the cake mixture curdles while adding the eggs to the creamed butter and sugar, stir in a tablespoon of flour and then continue to beat in the rest of the eggs.

Rich Chocolate Fudge Sauce Cake

Sinfully rich, this delicious melt-in-the-mouth chocolate cake has a crisp, almost meringue crust, and a soft, creamy, sauce-like consistency in the centre. Perfect as a dessert cake or with coffee, it will keep well for 3–4 days. Do not refrigerate or freeze; just cover the cake with aluminium foil while it is still in the cake pan.

2 TABLESPOONS BUTTER, FOR GREASING

250 G (8 OZ) BUTTER

250 G (8 OZ) EXCELLENT QUALITY DARK (SEMI-SWEET) CHOCOLATE, CHOPPED IN COARSE PIECES

¾ CUP (6 OZ) CASTER (SUPERFINE) SUGAR

4 TABLESPOONS (LIGHT) BROWN SUGAR

6 EGGS, SEPARATED

3 TABLESPOONS PLAIN (ALL-PURPOSE) FLOUR

3 TABLESPOONS GROUND ALMONDS

½ TEASPOON CREAM OF TARTAR

ICING (CONFECTIONERS') SUGAR, FOR DUSTING

1 CUP (8 FL OZ) CREAM, WHIPPED

A FEW DROPS OF VANILLA ESSENCE (EXTRACT)

1 TABLESPOON ICING (CONFECTIONERS') SUGAR, SIFTED

Preheat the oven to 180°C (350°F). Butter the sides and bottom of a 25 cm (9 in) springform pan with the 2 tablespoons butter. Line the bottom with baking paper (parchment) and flour the pan.

Melt the 250 g butter in a large, heavy saucepan. Add the chocolate, stirring constantly over low heat until the chocolate has just melted and the mixture is smooth. It should not get much hotter than 50°C (120°F). Set aside.

Beat the sugars into the egg yolks until just mixed. While the chocolate is still warm, whisk the egg mixture into it, then stir in the flour and almonds. If the combined mixture has cooled, warm it over low heat, stirring constantly, until it is barely warm.

Warm the egg whites slightly by swirling them in a bowl above a gas flame or over hot water. Add the cream of tartar to the egg whites and beat until they form rounded peaks. Fold the whites into the base mixture without deflating the whites.

Pour the batter into the cake pan and bake for 35–45 minutes or until the cake is completely set around the sides but still has a soft and creamy circle, about 12 cm (5 in) across, in the centre. The cake should tremble in the centre just slightly when you shake the pan gently. Cool thoroughly in the pan.

To serve, dust the cake with the icing sugar. Serve with the softly whipped cream flavoured with the vanilla and icing sugar.

SERVES 8–10

Gem Scones

If you have inherited some old gem irons, you'll probably be a dab hand at these light, tender cakes. Or have you forgotten how lovely they are?

30 G (1 OZ) BUTTER

2 TABLESPOONS SUGAR

1 EGG

A PINCH OF SALT

½ CUP (4 FL OZ) MILK

1 CUP (4 OZ) SELF-RAISING (SELF-RISING) FLOUR, SIFTED

Preheat the oven to 200°C (400°F) and use it to heat the gem irons.

Beat the butter and sugar to a cream. Add the egg, salt and milk and combine with the creamed mixture. Lightly fold in the flour until mixed. Have the irons very hot and grease them well. Three-quarters fill the gem irons with the batter. Bake for 10–15 minutes. Serve warm with fresh butter.

MAKES 10–12

Rich Chocolate Fudge Sauce Cake firms as it cools over several hours. The melt-in-the-mouth quality depends on it not being put in the refrigerator, even if it is not eaten the first day.

Griestorte

This light torte was particularly popular with the customers in London's Marylebone Lane Cordon Bleu restaurant, especially when served with plum or raspberry sauce.

3 EGGS, SEPARATED
½ CUP (4 OZ) CASTER (SUPERFINE) SUGAR
GRATED RIND AND JUICE OF 1 LEMON
4 TABLESPOONS FINE-GROUND SEMOLINA
1 TABLESPOON GROUND ALMONDS
1¼ CUPS (10 FL OZ) (LIGHT WHIPPING) CREAM,
　　WHIPPED
ICING (CONFECTIONERS') SUGAR, FOR DUSTING
FRESH FRUIT SUCH AS SLICED PLUMS, APRICOTS,
　　BERRIES, KIWI FRUIT, TO DECORATE

Preheat the oven to 180°C (350°F). Grease a 20 cm (8 in) sandwich tin (shallow round cake pan) and line with greased baking paper (parchment). Sprinkle the pan with a little caster sugar, then flour.

Beat the egg yolks and sugar until thick and creamy. Add the lemon rind and juice, beating until combined. Fold in the semolina and ground almonds. Beat the egg whites separately until stiff, and gently fold into the batter. Turn the batter into the prepared tin and bake for 30–40 minutes or until the cake leaves the sides of the pan. Remove from the oven and leave it for a few minutes before turning it out onto a wire rack to cool.

To serve, split the cake and fill it with half the whipped cream. Dust the top with icing sugar, then decorate with the remaining cream piped in rosettes. Top the cream with the fresh fruit and serve with a fruit sauce.

Fruit Sauce. If using plums or apricots, halve 250 g (8 oz) of them and remove the stones (pits). Dissolve ½ cup (4 oz) sugar in 1 cup (9 fl oz) water over heat and add the fruit. Poach gently until tender. Remove from heat and rub through a fine sieve. Allow to cool.

If using fresh berries, simply rub through a sieve and sweeten with a little icing sugar.

SERVES 8

Almond and Walnut Galette

This French cake—flattish, as a galette should be— is one of the more delicious and unusual nut cakes.

200 G (7 OZ) UNSALTED BUTTER
¾ CUP (6 OZ) CASTER (SUPERFINE) SUGAR
3 LARGE EGGS
2 CUPS (7 OZ) GROUND ALMONDS
2 CUPS (7 OZ) GROUND WALNUTS
½ CUP (2 OZ) PLAIN (ALL-PURPOSE) FLOUR
ICING (CONFECTIONERS') SUGAR, FOR DUSTING

Preheat the oven to 230°C (450°F). Butter a 25 cm (10 in) straight-edged flan ring (quiche pan) or cake pan, preferably with a loose bottom. Line the bottom with baking paper (parchment).

Cream the butter and beat in the sugar until light and fluffy. Add the eggs, one at a time, beating well after each addition. Stir in the nuts and flour, mixing gently but firmly. Turn the batter into the prepared pan and spread evenly. Bake for 12–15 minutes. Unmould and cool. Dust with sifted icing sugar. As this cake is rather rich, cut it into fairly thin wedges to serve.

SERVES 8–10

When testing a cake after the suggested cooking time, lightly press the surface with the tip of a finger. If the cake is cooked, the surface will spring back. The cake also will have shrunk from the sides of the pan. After the cake is cooked, it should be turned out onto a rack immediately unless the recipe specifies otherwise. The paper lining should be removed and the cake allowed to cool. Store in an airtight container until ready to serve.

Rich Chocolate Cake

A rich and absolutely superb chocolate cake. Serve it as a finale to an elegant meal with raspberries and sliced strawberries soaked in a little orange juice and rind, or liqueur.

375 G (12 OZ) DARK (SEMI-SWEET) COOKING
    CHOCOLATE, BROKEN INTO SMALL PIECES
60 G (2 OZ) UNSALTED BUTTER
⅔ CUP (2 OZ) PECAN OR WALNUT HALVES
4 TABLESPOONS PLAIN (ALL-PURPOSE) FLOUR
4 TABLESPOONS SUGAR
4 TABLESPOONS MANDARINE NAPOLEON LIQUEUR OR
    ORANGE-FLAVOURED LIQUEUR
3 TABLESPOONS WATER
6 LARGE EGGS, SEPARATED
A PINCH OF CREAM OF TARTAR

Preheat the oven to 180°C (350°F). Butter and flour a 25 cm (10 in) round cake pan.

Melt the chocolate and the butter in a small bowl placed over a saucepan of hot water. Stir until the mixture is smooth. In a food processor or blender, grind the nuts with the flour and sugar to a fine powder. Combine this with two-thirds of the chocolate mixture, liqueur and 3 tablespoons water.

Beat the egg yolks until thick and stir into the chocolate mixture. Beat the egg whites with the cream of tartar until soft peaks hold. Stir a spoonful into the mixture and when well blended fold in the remaining whites quickly and lightly with a large metal spoon. Pour the batter into the prepared pan and bake for 30 minutes, until firm and a skewer inserted comes out clean. Cool the cake in the pan on a rack for 20 minutes before turning it out.

The cake will sink considerably because it has so little flour and so many egg whites. Don't be alarmed by this. Gently reheat the reserved chocolate mixture, adding a little more chocolate if you feel this won't cover the cake. Once melted, glossy and smooth, spread over the cake, then cool. It is best not put in the refrigerator, as this can dull the glaze.

SERVES 8–10

Margaret's Chocolate Cake

This is a delicious chocolate cake, rich and moist with a coating of buttery almonds. It is a versatile cake, good for picnics, afternoon teas and parties.

15 G (½ OZ) BUTTER
4 TABLESPOONS FLAKED (SLICED) ALMONDS
1 CUP (8 FL OZ) BOILING WATER
125 G (4 OZ) DARK (SEMI-SWEET) CHOCOLATE,
    BROKEN INTO SMALL PIECES
1 TEASPOON BICARBONATE OF SODA (BAKING SODA)
250 G (8 OZ) UNSALTED BUTTER
1½ CUPS (11 OZ) CASTER (SUPERFINE) SUGAR
3 LARGE EGGS, SEPARATED
1 TEASPOON VANILLA ESSENCE (EXTRACT)
2½ CUPS (10 OZ) PLAIN (ALL-PURPOSE) FLOUR
A PINCH OF SALT
1 TEASPOON BAKING POWDER
⅔ CUP (5 FL OZ) LIGHT (DAIRY) SOUR CREAM

Preheat the oven to 180°C (350°F). Using the 15 g butter, generously butter a 12-cup bundt pan or two 20 cm (8 in) fluted ring tins (cake moulds). Sprinkle with the flaked almonds, pressing them well into the butter to coat the bottom and sides of the pan.

Put the boiling water, chocolate and bicarbonate of soda in a bowl and stir until smooth. Cream the 250 g butter and sugar until light, add the egg yolks one at a time, beating well after each addition. Stir in the vanilla then add the chocolate mixture a little at a time. Sift the flour, salt and baking powder and fold in alternately with the sour cream, mixing lightly until just combined. Beat the egg whites until stiff and fold into the batter with a large metal spoon.

Turn the batter gently into the prepared pan or tins, and bake in the oven—for 1–1¼ hours for the large cake, 45 minutes for the small cakes, or until cooked when tested with a skewer. Leave in the pan for a minute, then turn out and cool on a wire rack.

SERVES 10–12

Vacherin

This meringue dessert cake is a specialty of Alsace in France. It is fabulous filled with whipped cream and sliced strawberries or raspberries; a wonderful alternative is sweetened chestnut purée with whipped cream and vanilla folded through. For the fruit-filled vacherin, serve a sauce or coulis (page 164) made of the same fruit. The chestnut vacherin can be served plain or with a chocolate sauce.

1 QUANTITY MERINGUE MIXTURE (PAGE 167)
CASTER (SUPERFINE) SUGAR, FOR DUSTING
ICING (CONFECTIONER'S) SUGAR, FOR DUSTING
GLACÉ (CANDIED) CHESTNUTS, TO DECORATE
   (OPTIONAL)
FRUIT FILLING
1 CUP (8 FL OZ) (LIGHT WHIPPING) CREAM
1 PUNNET (250 G/8 OZ) RASPBERRIES OR SLICED
   STRAWBERRIES
CHESTNUT FILLING
½ CUP (4 FL OZ) (LIGHT WHIPPING) CREAM
½ CUP (4 FL OZ) SWEETENED CHESTNUT PURÉE

Trace two circles 23 cm (9 in) in diameter onto baking paper (parchment). Turn the paper over onto baking trays (sheets). Fill a piping (pastry) bag fitted with a plain 1 cm (½ in) tube (nozzle) with half the meringue mixture and pipe it onto one of the circles. Start from the centre and work round in a spiral shape to the outside edge of the circle. Cover the other circle with the remaining meringue mixture. Dust with a little caster (superfine) sugar and bake in a slow oven (120°C/250°F) for 1–1½ hours until the meringue is quite dry. If the meringue is moist underneath, turn it over and leave in the oven to dry out.

When the meringues are cool, cover one round with the filling of your choice and put the other round on top. Dust the top of the Vacherin with sifted icing sugar.
Fruit Filling. Whip the cream and fold in the berries.
Chestnut Filling. Whip the cream and fold it through the chestnut purée.

SERVES 8–10

Linzertorte

Most recipes for this torte from Linz in Austria call for a pastry with either almonds or hazelnuts. This version, because of its high nut content, is very short and melt-in-the-mouth. Because the mixture is so light, the lattice is piped over the top. The conserve filling could be sour cherry or plum instead of raspberry.

185 G (6 OZ) UNSALTED BUTTER
1 CUP (7 OZ) CASTER (SUPERFINE) SUGAR
GRATED RIND OF 1 LEMON OR ½ TEASPOON VANILLA
   ESSENCE (EXTRACT)
2 EGGS
1¼ CUPS (5 OZ) PLAIN (ALL-PURPOSE) FLOUR
½ TEASPOON GROUND CINNAMON
1¼ CUPS (4 OZ) GROUND ALMONDS
⅔ CUP (6 FL OZ) RASPBERRY CONSERVE
ICING (CONFECTIONERS') SUGAR, FOR DUSTING

Preheat the oven to 160°C (325°F). Lightly butter a 23 cm (9 in) round pan with a removable base (cheesecake pan).

Cream the butter with the sugar. Beat in the rind or vanilla with the eggs, adding one at a time. Sift the flour with the cinnamon and fold into the creamed mixture with the ground almonds until well mixed.

Spoon a third of the batter into a piping bag fitted with a plain 5 mm (¼ in) tube (nozzle). Spread the remaining batter in the prepared pan. Gently spread the raspberry conserve over the top, leaving an edge of 2.5 cm (1 in) free.

Pipe a ring of batter around the inside edge of the cake pan, then use the remaining batter to pipe a lattice over the top, not too close together. Bake for 30–40 minutes until golden and firm. Leave to cool in the pan for a few minutes before removing (with the base) from the pan and cooling on a wire rack. The torte may be served warm or cooled, dusted with icing sugar.

SERVES 8–10

Linzertorte is made with a pastry so light that it has to be spread and piped rather than rolled.

Gâteau Progrès

*Here is a cake that lives up to its name, something
to help celebrate a special achievement in one's life.
There are three basic steps in its preparation: first, the
making of the nut meringue layers; second, the making
of the butter cream; and third, the layering together
and finishing off. The first two steps can be done well
ahead of time, and the finishing off can be done a few
hours before the cake is needed.*

*It is traditional to dredge the top with icing sugar
and pipe 'Progrès' across the centre of the cake, though
it wasn't done for our photograph. The two methods
of finishing the cake are given here.*

¾ CUP (6 OZ) CASTER (SUPERFINE) SUGAR

1¼ CUPS (4 OZ) GROUND ALMONDS

5 EGG WHITES

3 DROPS VANILLA ESSENCE (EXTRACT)

1 QUANTITY COFFEE BUTTER CREAM (PAGE 164)

½ CUP PRALINE (PAGE 170) (OPTIONAL)

ALMONDS, BLANCHED, TOASTED AND CHOPPED, TO
    DECORATE

ICING (CONFECTIONERS') SUGAR, FOR DUSTING

Have ready three baking trays (sheets), each
lined with baking paper (parchment) on
which has been marked a 20 cm (8 in) circle.
Preheat the oven to 180°C (350°).

Sift the sugar, reserving 3 tablespoons, and
ground almonds together. Whisk the egg
whites (preferably in a copper bowl, but an
electric mixer will do) until stiff peaks form,
but the mixture is not dry. Beat in the
3 tablespoons of reserved sugar until the
mixture is thick and glossy. Fold in the sifted
sugar and almond mixture quickly and lightly.

Divide the mixture into three portions and
spread on the baking paper circles neatly.

Bake for about 20 minutes or until firm to
the touch. Remove to wire racks to cool.
Meanwhile, set aside a little less than half the
Coffee Butter Cream and flavour the rest
with Praline if using.

When the meringue rounds are cool, lay
one on a serving plate and spread with half
the praline-flavoured Coffee Butter Cream.

Lay the second round on top and spread with
the remaining praline-flavoured butter
cream. Top with the last round of meringue
and cover the sides only of the cake with the
reserved Coffee Butter Cream, keeping a
little aside if you are going to pipe the top.
Press the toasted almonds into the butter
cream at the sides and dust the top of the
cake with icing sugar. Finish by piping
'Progrès' on top.

Alternatively, cover the sides and top of the
cake with the remaining Coffee Butter Cream.
Cover the entire cake with the browned
almonds. Dust with icing sugar.

SERVES 8–10

*For a lighter, spongier cake, the flour and salt
are sifted three times and gently folded into the
egg mixture lightly and evenly. Never beat
the flour in, as this will give a tough sponge.
Always use a metal spoon or spatula or your
hand for folding in the flour.*

Kugelhopf

One of the lovely continental cakes, always to be found in the nicest cake shops. Eat it warm and fresh with coffee.

15 G (½ OZ) BUTTER

½ CUP (2 OZ) SLIVERED ALMONDS

1 CUP (6 OZ) SULTANAS (GOLDEN RAISINS)

3 TABLESPOONS RUM

¾ CUP (6 FL OZ) MILK

30 G (1 OZ) COMPRESSED (FRESH) YEAST

3 CUPS (12 OZ) PLAIN (ALL-PURPOSE) FLOUR

A PINCH OF SALT

½ TEASPOON GRATED LEMON RIND

1½ TABLESPOONS CASTER (SUPERFINE) SUGAR

3 EGGS, SLIGHTLY BEATEN

125 G (4 OZ) BUTTER, MELTED AND SLIGHTLY
    COOLED

ICING (CONFECTIONERS') SUGAR, FOR DUSTING

Generously butter a 20 cm (8 in) fluted ring tin (cake mould) and press the slivered almonds into the butter. Refrigerate until needed.

Soak the sultanas in the rum. Warm the milk until just at blood temperature, pour it onto the yeast and stir until dissolved.

Sift the flour and the salt into a warm bowl and sprinkle the lemon rind over. Make a well in the centre and pour in the milk and yeast mixture, sugar, eggs and melted butter. Mix thoroughly and add the sultanas. Spoon the batter into the prepared tin until it is three-quarters full. Stand in a warm place for 20–30 minutes or until the batter has risen to 2.5 cm (1 in) below the top of the tin. Bake in a preheated oven at 190°C (375°F) for 50–60 minutes.

When cooked, let the cake stand a few minutes before turning it out onto a wire rack to cool. Dust with icing sugar.

SERVES 8

Glazed Lemon and Buttermilk Cake

This cake has a marvellously refreshing lemon tang.

250 G (8 OZ) UNSALTED BUTTER, AT ROOM
    TEMPERATURE

1½ CUPS (12 OZ) CASTER (SUPERFINE) SUGAR

3 EGGS

3 CUPS (12 OZ) PLAIN (ALL-PURPOSE) FLOUR

½ TEASPOON BICARBONATE OF SODA (BAKING SODA)

½ TEASPOON SALT

1 CUP (8 FL OZ) BUTTERMILK

2 TABLESPOONS GRATED LEMON RIND

2 TABLESPOONS LEMON JUICE

LEMON GLAZE

60 G (2 OZ) UNSALTED BUTTER, SOFTENED

1¼ CUPS (7 OZ) ICING (CONFECTIONERS') SUGAR,
    SIFTED

2 TABLESPOONS GRATED LEMON RIND

3 TABLESPOONS LEMON JUICE

Preheat the oven to 160°C (325°F) and butter a 25 cm (10 in) ring tin (tube pan).

Cream the butter until softened and beat in the sugar until light and fluffy. Beat in the eggs, one at a time.

Sift the flour with the bicarbonate of soda and salt. Fold into the creamed mixture alternately with the buttermilk, lemon rind and juice. When combined, turn the batter into the prepared cake tin. Bake in the centre of the oven for 1 hour or until a fine skewer inserted comes out clean and the cake pulls away slightly from the edges. Leave the cake to cool in the tin on a wire rack for 10 minutes before carefully turning out. Spread with lemon glaze while still hot.

Lemon glaze. Cream the butter and sugar until light and fluffy. Gradually mix in the lemon rind and juice.

SERVES 8–10

Carrot Cake with Cream Cheese Frosting

This is the best carrot cake recipe I've tried, yet it is so simple to make. A simpler icing can be used instead of the cream cheese frosting. If you want to decorate it with marzipan figures, see page 132.

3 CUPS (12 OZ) PLAIN (ALL-PURPOSE) FLOUR

1½ CUPS (11 OZ) CASTER (SUPERFINE) SUGAR

1 TEASPOON SALT

1½ TEASPOONS BICARBONATE OF SODA (BAKING SODA)

1 CUP (8 FL OZ) CANNED CRUSHED PINEAPPLE, UNDRAINED

2 CUPS (12 OZ) GRATED CARROT

4 EGGS

1½ CUPS (12 FL OZ) SALAD OIL

1 TEASPOON VANILLA ESSENCE (EXTRACT)

1 CUP (4 OZ) CHOPPED WALNUTS

CREAM CHEESE FROSTING

1 CUP (6 OZ) ICING (CONFECTIONERS') SUGAR, SIFTED

125 G (4 OZ) CREAM CHEESE, SOFTENED

GRATED LEMON OR ORANGE RIND, OR VANILLA ESSENCE (EXTRACT) OR CITRUS JUICE FOR FLAVOURING

Preheat the oven to 180°C (350°F). Butter and line two 20 cm (8 in) sandwich tins (shallow round cake pans).

Sift the flour, sugar, salt and bicarbonate of soda together into a large mixing bowl. Add the pineapple, carrot, eggs, oil and vanilla and beat until combined. Stir in the chopped nuts. Spoon the batter into the prepared tins. Bake for 1 hour or until a skewer inserted in the centre comes out clean. Turn out to cool on wire racks.

Cream Cheese Frosting. Gradually beat the icing sugar into the cream cheese until light and fluffy. Add a little grated lemon or orange rind, vanilla essence or citrus juice to flavour.

When the cakes are cool, sandwich them together with half the Cream Cheese Frosting and spread the remaining frosting on top.

SERVES 8–10

Cider Pumpkin Bread

This quick bread will keep, well wrapped, for up to a week. If stored in the freezer, it will keep for several months.

1 CUP (8 FL OZ) APPLE CIDER

2 EGGS

3 TABLESPOONS VEGETABLE OIL

1 CUP (8 FL OZ) PUMPKIN PURÉE

¾ CUP (4 OZ) FIRMLY PACKED (LIGHT) BROWN SUGAR

2 TABLESPOONS GRATED ORANGE RIND

2 CUPS (8 OZ) PLAIN (ALL-PURPOSE) FLOUR

2 TEASPOONS BAKING POWDER

½ TEASPOON SALT

¼ TEASPOON BICARBONATE OF SODA (BAKING SODA)

¼ TEASPOON EACH MACE AND CINNAMON

4 TABLESPOONS CHOPPED WALNUTS OR PECANS

Preheat the oven to 180°C (350°F). Generously butter a 20 x 10 x 5 cm (8 x 4 x 2 in) loaf pan.

In a medium saucepan, reduce the apple cider over a high heat to 3 tablespoons.

Beat the eggs in a bowl with the oil, pumpkin purée and sugar. Add the cider and the orange rind, and beat the mixture until well combined. In another bowl, sift the flour with the baking powder, salt, bicarbonate of soda and spices, and fold into the pumpkin mixture until just combined.

Stir in the nuts and turn the batter into the prepared loaf pan. Bake for 1 hour or until a skewer inserted in the centre comes out clean. Remove from the oven and leave to cool completely in the pan placed on a rack before turning out.

SERVES 8–10

Carrot Cake with Cream Cheese Frosting becomes a child's fantasy when decorated with marzipan rabbits and carrots (page 132).

Stollen

This German Christmas cake is rich with butter, eggs, almonds and rum-macerated fruits. It improves with keeping, as the fruits help to moisten the dry dough. It is almost as good cut into slices and toasted, which is useful to remember when it becomes too dry.

2 STRIPS OF ANGELICA

4 TABLESPOONS EACH RAISINS, CURRANTS AND
  GLACÉ (CANDIED) CHERRIES, HALVED

⅔ CUP (4 OZ) CHOPPED MIXED (CANDIED) PEEL

4 TABLESPOONS RUM

½ CUP (2 OZ) SLIVERED ALMONDS

4 CUPS (1 LB) PLAIN (ALL-PURPOSE) FLOUR

A LARGE PINCH OF SALT

4 TABLESPOONS MILK, WARMED

30 G (1 OZ) COMPRESSED (FRESH) YEAST

125 G (4 OZ) BUTTER

½ CUP (4 OZ) CASTER (SUPERFINE) SUGAR

2 EGGS, LIGHTLY BEATEN

MELTED BUTTER, FOR BRUSHING

ICING (CONFECTIONERS') SUGAR, SIFTED, FOR
  DUSTING

Cut the strips of angelica into dice. Place them with the fruit and peel in a bowl, and pour over the rum. Toss well and allow to stand, covered, for 2 hours or preferably overnight. Drain and dry the fruit well on kitchen paper towels and toss them in a little flour.

Sift the flour with the salt into a bowl. Place the milk in a bowl, add the yeast and butter and stir until the yeast has dissolved, then mix in the sugar and eggs.

Make a well in the centre of the flour, pour in the yeast mixture and mix until smooth, commencing with a wooden spoon and finishing off with the hand. When the dough leaves the sides of the bowl, turn onto a lightly floured board and knead until smooth and elastic—this may take 10–15 minutes.

Place the dough into a clean greased bowl, cover with a damp cloth and leave in a warm place until doubled in size—for about 50 minutes to 1 hour.

Knock back (punch) down the dough and shape it into a square. Spoon the prepared fruits and the almonds into the middle of the square. Fold the dough over the fruits and nuts; knead them lightly into the dough. Place into a greased bowl, cover and leave in a warm place to rise for 30–45 minutes.

Knock (punch) the dough down and roll it out on a floured board into a 38 x 23 cm (15 x 9 in) oblong. Fold the short sides into the middle, each edge overlapping the centre by about 2.5 cm (1 in). Press the edges gently together to keep them in place. With lightly floured hands, taper the ends slightly and pat the sides to form a mound in the centre. The finished loaf should be about 8 cm (3 in) wide. Place on a greased tray (sheet), brush with a little melted butter and stand in a warm place for about 1 hour or until doubled in bulk.

Bake in a preheated oven at 190°C (375°F) for about 45 minutes or until golden brown and crusty. Cool on a wire rack. Dust heavily with icing sugar before slicing and buttering.

SERVES 10–12

To whip cream for decorating and piping, make sure it is icy cold. Chill the bowl and the beaters or whisk, and stand the bowl over ice while beating. These precautions are very important in summer. Well-chilled cream beats to a stiff consistency without becoming grainy, whereas unchilled cream has a tendency to curdle before stiffening. It's an idea to chill the piping bag and nozzle too, or run them under cold water just before using.

Maids of Honour

These little tartlets are said to have been the favourites of Anne Boleyn and her maids of honour. There are many versions of the recipe, though they all have a cheese and lemon filling.

1 QUANTITY RICH SHORTCRUST PASTRY (PAGE 161)

90 G (3 OZ) BUTTER, SOFTENED

200 G (7 OZ) CREAM CHEESE

4 TABLESPOONS CASTER (SUPERFINE) SUGAR

2 EGGS

3 TABLESPOONS BRANDY

3 TABLESPOONS GROUND ALMONDS

½ TEASPOON GROUND NUTMEG

GRATED RIND OF 2 LEMONS

JUICE OF 1 LEMON

Preheat the oven to 190°C (375°F). Roll the pastry out on a floured board and cut it into 24 circles using a 7.5 cm (3 in) cutter dipped in flour. Line 24 tartlet pans with these pastry circles.

In a mixing bowl soften and cream the butter and gradually beat in the cream cheese. Beat in the sugar and, when well incorporated, beat in the eggs and brandy. In another bowl, beat the almonds, nutmeg, lemon rind and juice together and gradually mix in the cream cheese mixture. Beat thoroughly and spoon into the pastry cases (shells).

Bake the tarts for 35–40 minutes until firm. Remove them from the oven and leave to cool a few minutes in their pans before removing to wire racks to cool completely.

MAKES 24 TARTLETS

Raspberry Powder Puffs

An old-fashioned recipe that came in handy on those occasions when the vicar was due to call. An hour before he was expected, these crisp little sponge cakes were taken out of their airtight containers, filled with whipped cream and jam, and put aside. By the time the vicar arrived they would have risen into light and tender puffs. From the dusting of icing sugar they earned their name—powder puffs. Don't wait for the vicar!

2 EGGS

½ CUP (4 OZ) CASTER (SUPERFINE) SUGAR

3 TABLESPOONS PLAIN (ALL-PURPOSE) FLOUR

3 TABLESPOONS CORNFLOUR (CORNSTARCH)

1 TEASPOON BAKING POWDER

½ CUP (5 OZ) RASPBERRY JAM

¾ CUP (6 FL OZ) CREAM, (LIGHT WHIPPING) WHIPPED

ICING (CONFECTIONERS') SUGAR, FOR DUSTING

Preheat the oven to 220°C (425°F). Grease and flour 3–4 baking trays (sheets).

Beat the eggs with an electric mixer until well mixed, then gradually add the sugar, beating for 10 minutes or until thick and creamy. Sift the flour, cornflour and baking powder together and fold in lightly.

Put the mixture into a piping (pastry) bag fitted with a plain 1 cm (½ in) tube (nozzle) and pipe into rounds, placing them well apart on the prepared trays. If you don't have a piping bag, spoon teaspoons of the mixture onto the trays.

Bake for 4–5 minutes until evenly but lightly coloured. Lift carefully onto a wire rack to cool. Store in an airtight container.

An hour or so before serving, join the cakes together in pairs with jam and whipped cream. Dust them with icing sugar and place them in a covered container until they become light puffs.

MAKES ABOUT 18

BISCUITS AND COOKIES

Biscuits and cookies, in their wondrous variety of shapes, sizes, flavours and textures, are often just the thing for certain occasions. They give the coffee break a special lift, creamy desserts a flourishing finish and they always make a visitor feel especially welcome.

There are simple drop biscuits, which are easily made and perfect for brightening up a cup of tea or coffee, or a lunchbox. Delicate and crisp biscuits like cigarettes russes, almond tuiles or brandy snaps add a special touch when served with creamy or fruit desserts, ices or afternoon teas.

Vanilla kippels from Austria, shortbread from Scotland, ricciarelli from Italy, sugar-glazed flaky pastry fingers from France—quite naturally a list of the most delectable biscuits is international in flavour. Some melt in the mouth, others are crisp, and then there are the hard biscotti from Italy for dunking in sweet wine or hot coffee. All have their moments.

Biscuit and Cookie Tips

Whether you know them as biscuits or as cookies, two baking trays (sheets) are necessary for most biscuit and cookie making, along with at least one metal-bladed spatula for removing biscuits from the tray.

One or two wire racks will be needed to ensure that the biscuits do not overlap when cooling.

Follow the instructions carefully as regards size when dropping the dough onto the trays —½ teaspoons, teaspoons and tablespoons mean exactly that. For another guide to size, refer to the quantities each recipe makes.

Some of the special biscuits, such as florentines, almond tuiles and brandy snaps, may spread alarmingly during cooking. If so, simply gather up the edges with a large biscuit (cookie) cutter to bring them back into their proper shape again, and return them to the oven to finish cooking. These biscuits may also be difficult to slide off the baking tray; I have found that using butter to grease the trays is the best way to prevent this. But it may be that the biscuits have cooled too quickly and stick like limpets to the tray, in which case a minute or so back in the oven will soften them sufficiently to allow them to be removed with ease.

For biscuit recipes, the egg used is 55 g (about 2 oz), and the butter is unsalted.

Always preheat the oven. The placement of the trays (sheets) during baking is important; heat should circulate around trays. During baking, turn the trays to compensate for uneven baking.

Grease baking trays (sheets) with unsalted fats, preferably butter. For delicate biscuits, use a special baking paper (parchment), from which they can be peeled when slightly cooled.

Baking trays (sheets) should always be cold when the uncooked biscuits are placed on them, so that the biscuits will not lose their shape when cooking.

Baked and cooled biscuits and cookies should always be stored in airtight containers. Fragile wafers should be stored in layers separated with foil or greaseproof (wax) paper.

Burnt Butter Biscuits

Burnt butter adds a special flavour to these lovely biscuits, but don't take the description literally.

125 G (4 OZ) BUTTER
½ CUP (4 OZ) CASTER (SUPERFINE) SUGAR
1 EGG
1 TEASPOON VANILLA ESSENCE (EXTRACT)
1½ CUPS (6 OZ) SELF-RAISING (SELF-RISING) FLOUR
A PINCH OF SALT
60 G (2 OZ) BLANCHED ALMONDS

Grease baking trays (sheets) and preheat the oven to 180°C (350°F).

Melt the butter in a saucepan and allow it to turn a light brown colour over a gentle heat. Cool slightly, add the sugar and beat well. Stir in the egg and vanilla. Fold in the sifted flour and salt.

Roll the dough into balls about the size of a small walnut. Place them on the prepared baking trays, allowing room for spreading. Place a blanched almond on top of each ball, then bake for 12–15 minutes.

MAKES 24

Flaky French Fingers

Simple light, flaky biscuits, perfect to serve with a dessert. When sandwiched together with butter cream, they can stand on their own on the tea or coffee tray.

2½ CUPS (10 OZ) PLAIN (ALL-PURPOSE) FLOUR
250 G (8 OZ) BUTTER
1 TABLESPOON VINEGAR
4 TABLESPOONS WATER
⅓–½ CUP (3–4 OZ) SUGAR

BUTTER CREAM
185 G (6 OZ) BUTTER
½ CUP (3 OZ) ICING (CONFECTIONERS') SUGAR
1 EGG YOLK
VANILLA ESSENCE (EXTRACT), TO TASTE

Sift the flour into a bowl and rub in the butter with your fingertips until the mixture resembles breadcrumbs. Add the vinegar to the water and sprinkle it over the dry mixture, 1 tablespoon at a time, while tossing with a fork. Continue to add the water mixture until the dough is just moist enough to hold together. Divide the dough into 2 balls, wrap in plastic wrap (cling film) and chill for 20 minutes.

Preheat the oven to 230°C (450°F). Roll out the dough on a lightly floured surface to 6 mm (¼ in) thickness. Cut into oblong shapes 7.5 x 2.5 cm (3 x 1 in). Place the sugar on greaseproof (wax) paper and press the top of each biscuit shape on so that the sugar clings to it. Transfer, sugar side up, to ungreased baking trays (sheets) and bake for 8–10 minutes, or until the top begins to caramelise. Roll and cook the remaining dough in the same way. Cool completely on wire racks and store in an airtight container.

Butter Cream. Beat butter to a soft cream. Beat in the icing sugar, then add the egg yolk and vanilla. Beat until light, smooth and creamy.

MAKES 48 SINGLE, 24 DOUBLE

Vanilla Kippels

Very European, little almond shortbread crescents to serve with coffee or with a fruit or ice cream dessert.

1¼ CUPS (5 OZ) PLAIN (ALL-PURPOSE) FLOUR
A PINCH OF SALT
155 G (5 OZ) BUTTER
3 TABLESPOONS ICING (CONFECTIONERS') SUGAR
2 EGG YOLKS
½ TEASPOON VANILLA ESSENCE (EXTRACT)
1¼ CUPS (5 OZ) GROUND ALMONDS
EXTRA ICING SUGAR, SIFTED, FOR DREDGING

Sift the flour with the salt on to a pastry board. Make a well in the centre and put in the butter, sugar, egg yolks and vanilla. Sprinkle the ground almonds onto the flour. Work the ingredients in the centre with your fingertips until thoroughly blended. Using a metal spatula, quickly draw in the flour and ground almonds. Knead the dough lightly until smooth, then form it into a ball. Wrap it in plastic wrap (cling film) and chill for 1 hour.

Preheat the oven to 180°C (350°F) and butter 2 baking trays (sheets). Divide the dough into walnut-size pieces and roll these into balls. In the palm of the hand roll each ball into a small cigar shape, then curve this into a crescent. Arrange the crescents on the prepared baking trays.

Bake for 10–12 minutes, until lightly coloured. Remove the biscuits to a wire rack and place a sheet of greaseproof (waxed) paper under the rack. Dredge the crescents heavily with the sifted icing sugar while they are still warm. Cool and store in an airtight container.

MAKES ABOUT 40

Pages 34–35: A fine selection of homemade biscuits. Clockwise from left: Cigarettes Russes, the perfect biscuit to serve with fruit or cream desserts; Austrian Jam Rings (on plate and in front); and rich and nutty Vanilla Kippels.

Austrian Jam Rings

Circles of light, crisp biscuit are sandwiched with a bright fruit jam. Pretty on a tea tray.

2 CUPS (8 OZ) PLAIN (ALL-PURPOSE) FLOUR
1 TEASPOON BAKING POWDER
¼ TEASPOON EACH GROUND CINNAMON AND CLOVES
½ CUP (4 OZ) SUGAR
RIND OF ½ LEMON, GRATED
185 G (6 OZ) UNSALTED BUTTER, SOFTENED
1 EGG
BLACKCURRANT, RASPBERRY OR APRICOT JAM
ICING (CONFECTIONERS') SUGAR, FOR DUSTING

Sift the flour and baking powder with the spices into a bowl. Stir in the sugar and lemon rind. Add the butter, then the egg. Mix well together to form a smooth dough and knead lightly on a well-floured board. Wrap in plastic wrap (cling film) and chill for 15 minutes.

Preheat the oven to 180°C (350°F) and butter two baking trays (sheets). Divide the dough into three. Roll out thinly on a floured board. Cut into rounds with a 5 cm (2 in) fluted cutter and, using a smaller fluted or heart-shaped cutter, remove the centre from half the biscuits.

Place on the prepared baking trays and bake for 8–10 minutes until pale golden. Cool on wire racks. Just before serving, heat the jam slightly and spoon a little on the plain biscuits. Place rings on top and dust with icing sugar.

MAKES ABOUT 20

Lemon Sponge Fingers have a fresh tart lemon sponge topping on a shortbread base.

Lemon Sponge Fingers

185 G (6 OZ) UNSALTED BUTTER
½ CUP (3 OZ) ICING (CONFECTIONERS') SUGAR, SIFTED
2 CUPS (8 OZ) PLAIN (ALL-PURPOSE) FLOUR
4 TABLESPOONS POTATO FLOUR
LEMON TOPPING
RIND OF 3 LEMONS, GRATED
1 CUP (7 OZ) CASTER (SUPERFINE) SUGAR
3 EGGS
4 TABLESPOONS PLAIN (ALL-PURPOSE) FLOUR
¾ TEASPOON BAKING POWDER
3 TABLESPOONS STRAINED LEMON JUICE
ICING (CONFECTIONERS') SUGAR, SIFTED, FOR DUSTING

Preheat the oven to 180°C (350°F).

Cream the butter in a medium bowl until soft. Gradually beat in the icing sugar until the mixture is light and fluffy. Sift the flours into the mixture and mix together, using a spatula or knife, to form a soft dough. Spread this shortbread dough evenly in the base of a 33 x 23 cm (13 x 9 in) Swiss roll tin (jelly roll pan). If necessary, smooth it out with the back of a spoon, having first covered the dough with a sheet of plastic wrap (cling film). Remove the wrap, prick the dough all over with a fork and chill for 30 minutes. Bake for 15–20 minutes until pale golden, then remove from the oven. Leave the oven on.

Lemon Topping. Place the grated lemon rind, sugar and eggs in a bowl. Whisk together until a pale and thick cream. Sift in the flour with the baking powder and fold this into the whisked mixture with the lemon juice.

When the topping is mixed, pour it over the prepared shortbread base and return it to the oven for 25 minutes until set and very lightly browned. Leave to cool in tin. When cold, cut the oblong into 3 even strips lengthwise and 10 across. Dust with sifted icing sugar to serve.

MAKES 30 FINGERS

Marbled Cheesecake Brownies

These brownies have a marvellous fudgy texture: cheesecake with a crispy top, marbled with chocolate and studded with pecans. The mixture is baked in a square, then cooled and cut into individual squares. Great for picnics, as a sweet finish to a barbecue or just with an ice-cold glass of milk at home.

60 G (2 OZ) BUTTER
125 G (4 OZ) CREAM CHEESE (PHILADELPHIA, NEUFCHÂTEL)
3 TABLESPOONS CASTER (SUPERFINE) SUGAR
1 EGG
1 TABLESPOON PLAIN (ALL-PURPOSE) FLOUR
½ TEASPOON VANILLA ESSENCE (EXTRACT)
CHOCOLATE MIXTURE
125 G (4 OZ) DARK (SEMI-SWEET) COOKING CHOCOLATE, ROUGHLY CHOPPED
90 G (3 OZ) BUTTER
2 EGGS
¾ CUP (6 OZ) CASTER (SUPERFINE) SUGAR
½ CUP (2 OZ) PLAIN (ALL-PURPOSE) FLOUR
¼ TEASPOON EACH BAKING POWDER AND SALT
½ CUP (2 OZ) COARSELY CHOPPED PECANS OR WALNUTS

Preheat the oven to 180°C (350°F) and butter a shallow 25 cm (10 in) square cake pan.

Cream the butter with the cream cheese. Gradually beat in the sugar until the mixture is light and fluffy. Add the egg and beat in thoroughly. Stir in the flour and vanilla essence and set aside.

Chocolate Mixture. Melt the chocolate and butter in a bowl over hot water, stirring constantly; cool. Beat the eggs until thick and pale, gradually beating in the sugar. Sift in the flour, baking powder and salt, then blend in the cooled chocolate mixture and pecans.

Measure 1 cup (8 fl oz) of chocolate batter and set aside. Spread the remaining chocolate batter in the prepared pan. Top with the reserved cheese mixture, then drop spoonfuls of the reserved chocolate batter on top. Swirl a knife through the batter to make a marbled pattern. Bake for 40–45 minutes. Remove from the oven and leave to cool in the pan before cutting into 5 cm (2 in) squares.

MAKES 25 SQUARES

Cardamom Cookies

A simple biscuit with the warm fragrance of cardamom.

125 G (4 OZ) BUTTER
1 TEASPOON BICARBONATE OF SODA (BAKING SODA)
1 TEASPOON GROUND CARDAMOM
¼ TEASPOON SALT
1 CUP (8 OZ) (LIGHT) BROWN SUGAR, FIRMLY PACKED
1 EGG
2 CUPS (8 OZ) PLAIN (ALL-PURPOSE) FLOUR, SIFTED
1 TEASPOON CREAM OF TARTAR

Cream the butter and add the bicarbonate of soda, cardamom and salt; mix well. Gradually beat in the sugar until the mixture is light and fluffy. Beat in the egg. Sift together the flour and cream of tartar and gradually stir into the butter mixture. Chill the dough until stiff enough to handle, 3–4 hours.

Preheat the oven to 180°C (350°F). Scoop out teaspoonfuls of the chilled dough and shape them into small balls. Place them on ungreased baking trays (sheets). Use a wetted fork to press each cookie into a round shape. Bake for 15–18 minutes until light golden. Remove from the trays, cool and store in an airtight container.

MAKES ABOUT 45

Oat and Raisin Biscuits

These are good biscuits to have on hand at any time, with a cup of tea, as an after-school bite, in a lunch box or to carry along to a picnic.

250 G (8 OZ) BUTTER
1 CUP (6 OZ) (LIGHT) BROWN SUGAR
½ CUP (4 OZ) SUGAR
1 EGG
2 TEASPOONS VANILLA ESSENCE (EXTRACT)
2 CUPS (8 OZ) PLAIN (ALL-PURPOSE) FLOUR
½ TEASPOON SALT
½ TEASPOON BICARBONATE OF SODA (BAKING SODA)
1 TEASPOON GROUND CINNAMON
3 TABLESPOONS WATER
1 CUP (6 OZ) RAISINS
2½ CUPS (7 OZ) ROLLED OATS

Preheat the oven to 190°C (375°F) and butter two baking trays (sheets).

Cream the butter with the sugars and beat in the egg and vanilla essence until light and fluffy. Fold in the flour, sifted with the salt, bicarbonate of soda and cinnamon, and add the water, raisins and oats. Mix well and drop heaped teaspoons of the dough onto the prepared baking trays. Bake for 12–15 minutes or until lightly browned. Remove and cool on a wire rack.

MAKES 50–60

When removed from the oven, most biscuits are soft and should be left on the baking tray (sheet) for a few minutes to firm before being removed to a cooling rack. Biscuits such as Brandy Snaps and Cigarettes Russes, however, have to be removed quickly from the baking tray so that they can be shaped while still hot.

Orangines

Good health food stores or the food halls of large department stores should sell good-quality candied orange peel; otherwise substitute mixed peel to make these lovely, slightly chewy orange and almond biscuits.

60 G (2 OZ) UNSALTED BUTTER
3 TABLESPOONS CASTER (SUPERFINE) SUGAR
½ CUP (2 OZ) PLAIN (ALL-PURPOSE) FLOUR, SIFTED
⅓ CUP (2 OZ) BLANCHED ALMONDS, VERY FINELY CHOPPED
4 TABLESPOONS FINELY CHOPPED CANDIED ORANGE PEEL
2 TEASPOONS MILK

Preheat the oven to 180°C (350°F).

Cream the butter in a bowl, and beat in the sugar until thick and pale. Stir in the flour, almonds and peel, moistening with the milk.

Put teaspoonfuls of the dough onto a greased baking tray (sheet), flatten with a wet fork to 4 cm (1½ in) rounds and bake until tinged with brown, about 7–8 minutes. Leave to cool for 2–3 minutes before carefully removing them from the tray and cooling them completely on wire racks.

MAKES ABOUT 36

Follow the instructions carefully as regards size when dropping dough on baking trays (sheets) —½ teaspoons, teaspoons and tablespoons mean exactly that. For confirmation of the size, refer to the quantities each recipe makes.

Almond Bread

This is the delicious almond bread you often find in pretty cellophane packets in good delicatessens. Very simple to make at home. You first make an almond loaf, then slice it very thinly and bake it again to achieve the lovely thin wafers. Serve with fruit or creamy desserts or with coffee.

3 EGG WHITES
½ CUP (4 OZ) CASTER (SUPERFINE) SUGAR
1 CUP (4 OZ) PLAIN (ALL-PURPOSE) FLOUR, SIFTED
1 CUP (5 OZ) UNBLANCHED ALMONDS
1 TEASPOON VANILLA ESSENCE (EXTRACT)

Preheat the oven to 180°C (350°F). Beat the egg whites until stiff without being dry, then gradually beat in the sugar. Continue beating until the mixture is thick and glossy. Using a metal spoon, fold in the flour, almonds and vanilla essence, mixing well. Turn the batter into a well-buttered small loaf pan, preferably one that has a non-stick lining.

Bake for about 30 minutes until pale golden and firm to the touch. Leave to cool in the pan, then turn out and wrap in foil. Leave in the refrigerator overnight; this will help you cut thin, even slices. Next day, cut into thin slices and place on an ungreased baking tray (sheet). Bake in a preheated oven at 150°C (300°F) until pale golden and crisp. Cool and store in an airtight container.

MAKES PLENTY

Biscotti di Prato

These biscuits are a Tuscan favourite. Curiously hard, they will keep for months in an airtight container, ready at any time for dunking into a sweet wine or coffee.

1¼ CUPS (6 OZ) UNBLANCHED ALMONDS
125 G (4 OZ) PINE NUTS
4 CUPS (1 LB) PLAIN (ALL-PURPOSE) FLOUR
4 EGGS, BEATEN
1 TABLESPOON GRATED ORANGE RIND
1 TEASPOON VANILLA ESSENCE (EXTRACT)
½ TEASPOON BAKING POWDER
2 CUPS (14 OZ) CASTER (SUPERFINE) SUGAR
A PINCH OF SALT

Preheat the oven to 190°C (375°F). Butter a baking tray (sheet) and dust with flour.

Toast the almonds in the oven for a couple of minutes and chop them roughly with the pine nuts. Sift the flour onto a pastry board. Make a well in the middle and pour in the eggs, orange rind, vanilla, baking powder, sugar and salt. Work to a smooth consistency with your hands and then mix in the nuts. Divide the dough into three and roll each piece into a long loaf to fit the length of the baking tray.

Place the loaves on the prepared baking tray and bake for about 20 minutes. Remove and slice the loaves on the diagonal about 1 cm (½ in) thick. Bake on baking trays for another 20 minutes until lightly browned. Store in airtight containers.

MAKES PLENTY

Almond Bread (in front of basket) gives a lift to ice cream desserts. Behind are Biscotti di Prato from Tuscany.

Hazelnut Crescents

*One of the most beautiful biscuits, especially when
the hazelnuts are good and fresh. Walnuts may be
used in place of hazelnuts.*

1¼ CUPS (5 OZ) PLAIN (ALL-PURPOSE) FLOUR
2 TABLESPOONS CASTER (SUPERFINE) SUGAR
125 G (4 OZ) BUTTER
½ CUP (2 OZ) VERY FINELY CHOPPED HAZELNUTS
1 EGG YOLK
EXTRA CASTER (SUPERFINE) SUGAR, FOR DUSTING

Sift the flour into a bowl, stir in the sugar and
rub in the butter until the mixture resembles
coarse breadcrumbs. Mix in the nuts and stir
in the egg yolk to make a dough. Cover and
chill for 30 minutes.

Preheat the oven to 180°C (350°F) and
lightly butter two baking trays (sheets). Take
about 2 teaspoons of dough at a time, roll into
6 cm (2½ in) lengths and shape into crescents.
Place on the prepared baking trays and bake
for 12 minutes or until lightly coloured.
Remove the crescents and roll them in the
extra caster sugar while still warm. Cool on a
wire rack and store in an airtight container.

MAKES ABOUT 35

Ricciarelli

Delectable little almond biscuits from Italy.

2 CUPS (10 OZ) BLANCHED ALMONDS
¾ CUP (6 OZ) CASTER (SUPERFINE) SUGAR
¾ CUP (4 OZ) ICING (CONFECTIONERS') SUGAR,
    SIFTED
½ TEASPOON VANILLA ESSENCE (EXTRACT)
2 EGG WHITES
EXTRA ICING (CONFECTIONER'S) SUGAR, SIFTED,
    FOR DUSTING

Grind the almonds as finely as possible, using
a blender or food processor, or use 3 cups
(10 oz) ground almonds. In a blender or food
processor, pound the ground almonds with the
caster sugar until almost a paste.

Mix the icing sugar and vanilla essence into
the almond paste. Beat the egg whites until
frothy and fold them into the almond mixture.
Add a little more icing sugar if necessary to
make a stiff paste. Pinch off small pieces of
paste and form them into oval or large almond
shapes. Place on wire racks, cover loosely with
a cloth and leave in a dry place for about
24 hours to dry out a little.

Preheat the oven to 140°C (275°F). Arrange
the ricciarelli on baking trays (sheets) and
bake for 30–40 minutes, until dry but still
very pale. Remove to wire racks to cool and
dust with extra icing sugar before storing in
airtight containers.

MAKES ABOUT 50

*Care of equipment. Metal baking trays (sheets)
and metal cutters become rusty if they are not
dried well after washing. To prevent rust, put
the implements in a warm oven to dry before
storing them away.*

*Two baking trays (sheets) are necessary for
most biscuit making, along with at least one
metal-bladed spatula for removing the biscuits or
cookies from the tray. One or two wire racks will
be needed for cooling the biscuits, to allow them to
cool without overlapping.*

Scottish Shortbread

For real shortbread made as the Scots do, the dough must be kneaded for about 5 minutes until it becomes smooth and very buttery. Then it is pressed into a cake pan or directly onto a baking tray (sheet) into a rectangle or round and pricked or decorated. This makes a superb shortbread, crisp yet tender. If made ahead, recrisp the shortbread in a moderate oven (180°C/350°F) for 15 minutes before serving. For a lighter shortbread, replace ¼ cup (1 oz) of the flour with the same amount of rice flour.

300 G (10 OZ) BUTTER
½ CUP (4 OZ) CASTER (SUPERFINE) SUGAR
4 CUPS (1 LB) PLAIN (ALL-PURPOSE) FLOUR

Preheat the oven to 180°C (350°F). Butter two 20 cm (8 in) sandwich tins (shallow round cake pans) or two baking trays (sheets). Alternatively, line with baking paper (parchment).

Cream the butter until it resembles whipped cream, then add the sugar gradually, beating until the mixture is light and fluffy. Work in the flour gradually, then knead to form a dough. Divide the dough into 2 pieces and knead each into 2 rounds. Press into the prepared sandwich tins or onto the baking trays. With the heel of the hand, push the dough out until you have a 20 cm (8 in) circle and the dough is very smooth, then smooth over the surface and edge with a palette knife. Crimp edges by pressing the edge of the dough with a finger and then pinching the edge together. If using a sandwich tin, fork the edge for decoration.

Prick the surface of the shortbread with a fork. (This is done to release moisture as it cooks, making the shortbread crisp.) Bake in the centre of the oven for 10 minutes, then reduce the temperature to 150°C (300°F) and bake for a further 40 minutes. Remove from the oven and cool completely on wire racks.

To serve, be like the Scots and break it in good-sized pieces.

MAKES 2 CAKES

Sablés

The light, crisp and grainy texture of these lovely shortbreads gives them their name, sablé—a 'sanded' biscuit. Serve as dessert biscuits or on a tea tray.

1¼ CUPS (5 OZ) PLAIN (ALL-PURPOSE) FLOUR
A PINCH OF SALT
3 TABLESPOONS CASTER (SUPERFINE) SUGAR
½ CUP (2 OZ) GROUND ALMONDS
RIND OF 1 LEMON, FINELY GRATED
90 G (3 OZ) BUTTER
2 EGG YOLKS
ICING (CONFECTIONERS') SUGAR, SIFTED, FOR DUSTING

Butter several baking trays (sheets).

Sift the flour, salt and sugar into a bowl. Mix in the almonds and lemon peel. Rub in the butter until the mixture resembles fine breadcrumbs, then mix in the egg yolks to form a soft dough.

Roll out the dough thinly on a floured surface. Using a biscuit (cookie) cutter, cut 4 cm (1½ in) rounds from the dough. Alternatively, cut biscuits by hand with a knife or pastry wheel, cutting the dough into long strips 7.5 cm (3 in) wide, then cutting across the strips at 4.5 cm (1¾ in) intervals to form oblongs. Place them slightly apart on the prepared baking trays. Refrigerate for 30 minutes.

Preheat the oven to 180°C (350°F). Bake for 15–20 minutes until the sablés are very lightly browned. Using a palette knife, carefully remove them from the baking trays to wire racks to cool. When cold, dust very lightly with icing sugar.

MAKES 32

Correct storing is important. Allow biscuits to cool on a wire rack unless the recipe stipulates cooling on the tray. When the biscuits are cool, store them in an airtight container. If they lose their crispness, heat them in the oven at 150°C (300°F) for 5 minutes.

Almond Tuiles

The French have named these lacy almond biscuits 'tuiles' (tiles) because they resemble in shape the old-fashioned curved roof tiles of France.

90 G (3 OZ) UNSALTED BUTTER
4 TABLESPOONS CASTER (SUPERFINE) SUGAR
4 TABLESPOONS PLAIN (ALL-PURPOSE) FLOUR
A PINCH OF SALT
⅔ CUP (2½ OZ) SLIVERED OR FLAKED (SLICED)
   ALMONDS

Preheat the oven to 200°C (400°F) and butter two baking trays (sheets).

Cream the butter and beat in the sugar until the mixture is light and fluffy. Sift the flour with the salt and fold it into the creamed mixture with the almonds. Put teaspoons of the dough onto one prepared tray at a time, starting with 3 spoonfuls at first until you are used to removing and handling the hot biscuit quickly enough to shape it. Flatten the dough slightly with a wet spatula or knife and leave plenty of room for spreading on the tray.

Bake until golden, about 5 minutes. Remove the tray from the oven, leave the biscuits a few moments on the tray before sliding them off with a spatula and draping them over a rolling pin to give them their characteristic curved shape. Leave them for a few seconds, then carefully remove the tuiles to wire racks to finish cooling. Once cooled, store in airtight containers.

MAKES ABOUT 24

To test if the batter or dough for biscuits such as Cigarettes Russes or Brandy Snaps is of the correct consistency, bake one biscuit first. If it is too firm and hard to remove from the tray (sheet), add an extra 1–2 teaspoons of melted butter. If the batter or dough is too soft and difficult to handle, add 1–2 teaspoons of plain (all-purpose) flour.

Cigarettes Russes

The secret of these crisp, furled biscuits lies in the spreading of the batter to the proper size on the tray, and having nimble fingers when rolling them while they are still very hot from the oven. The technique is quickly mastered and the biscuit is worth the trouble.

2 EGG WHITES
½ CUP (4 OZ) CASTER (SUPERFINE) SUGAR
90 G (3 OZ) UNSALTED BUTTER, MELTED
2 OR 3 DROPS OF VANILLA ESSENCE (EXTRACT)
½ CUP (2 OZ) PLAIN (ALL-PURPOSE) FLOUR, SIFTED

Preheat the oven to 190°C (375°F). Brush two baking trays (sheets) with a little melted butter and dust lightly with a little sifted plain flour. Shake off excess.

Beat the egg whites and sugar with a whisk or fork until smooth (it doesn't have to thicken). Stir in the melted butter, vanilla and flour.

Place a teaspoon of batter onto a prepared tray and spread it with a metal spatula or the back of a spoon into an oblong about 10 x 6 cm (4 x 2½ in) with rounded corners. If you are a beginner, do two at a time; once you've mastered them you can fit a few more on the tray. Bake for about 5 minutes, until the biscuits are golden on the edges and coloured in the centres.

Remove them from the oven, cool a few seconds and remove them one at a time with a slice from the tray. Quickly roll the biscuit around the handle of a wooden spoon to form it into its characteristic cigarette shape. (Having a few wooden spoons is helpful for this.) Once the biscuit has cooled slightly, remove the handle. Finish cooling on a wire rack and store in an airtight container.

MAKES 18–24

A selection of delicate biscuits to serve after dinner or with dessert. Clockwise from top: Almond Tuiles and Tuile Cups (made from Cigarettes Russes batter), Cigarettes Russes, and Florentines.

Florentines

I have tested many recipes for this classic thin, crisp wafer of fruit and almonds with a chocolate top. This one was very successful and as good as any I've tasted. Take note: though the mixture will spread a great deal during cooking, it may be simply gathered with the aid of a biscuit (cookie) cutter into a neat round shape.

125 G (4 OZ) BUTTER
⅔ CUP (5 OZ) CASTER (SUPERFINE) SUGAR
2 TABLESPOONS HONEY
4 TABLESPOONS (LIGHT WHIPPING) CREAM
A PINCH OF SALT
GRATED RIND OF ½ LEMON
1⅔ CUPS (6 OZ) FLAKED (SLICED) ALMONDS
2 TABLESPOONS (1 OZ) CHOPPED MIXED (CANDIED)
    PEEL
125 G (4 OZ) DARK (SEMI-SWEET) CHOCOLATE

Preheat the oven to 180°C (350°F). Grease a baking tray (sheet) well with butter or line with baking paper (parchment).

Place the butter, sugar, honey, cream, salt and lemon rind in a saucepan and lightly boil, for about 5 minutes. Stir constantly, until thick and creamy, and leaving the sides of the pan.

Add the almonds and peel. Mix well, then remove from heat. Spoon tablespoons of the mixture, about four to a tray, and flatten them slightly with a wet spoon. Bake for about 6 minutes. The mixture will spread unevenly, so remove the tray from the oven and gather up the edges of the florentines with a 5 cm (2 in) biscuit (cookie) cutter to make them into a round, even shape. Return to the oven for a further 4 minutes. Allow to cool a few moments on the tray (reshape, if necessary, using the cutter). Remove with an egg slice (lifter) or metal spatula to a wire rack to cool.

Melt the chocolate over a bowl of hot water, beat until smooth, then spread over the flat side of each cooled biscuit. Using the prongs of a fork or a serrated plastic blade, mark the chocolate in wavy lines and leave to set. Store in an airtight container.

MAKES ABOUT 25

Brandy Snaps

These crisp, lacy, rolled wafers are often enjoyed filled with whipped cream with afternoon tea or unfilled to accompany a fruit dessert.

60 G (2 OZ) BUTTER
4 TABLESPOONS CASTER (SUPERFINE) SUGAR OR
    (LIGHT) BROWN SUGAR
4 TABLESPOONS GOLDEN SYRUP (LIGHT TREACLE)
½ CUP (2 OZ) PLAIN (ALL-PURPOSE) FLOUR
1 TEASPOON GROUND GINGER
GRATED RIND OF ½ LEMON
WHIPPED CREAM, FOR FILLING (OPTIONAL)

Preheat the oven to 180°C (350°F). Grease two baking trays (sheets).

Put the butter, sugar and golden syrup into a saucepan and heat very gently until the butter has melted. Remove from heat and cool until lukewarm. Sift in the flour with the ground ginger and stir in with the lemon rind.

Drop teaspoons of the batter (3 on each tray) on one tray at a time, allowing 5–7 cm (2–3 in) between each for spreading. Bake for 6–8 minutes. When the biscuits are golden brown, remove them from the oven, let them stand for a minute or so until they set a little, then ease them off the tray with a broad-bladed knife or metal spatula, using a gentle sawing motion. Working quickly, wrap each one lightly around the greased cylindrical handle of a wooden spoon (the larger the better), keeping the smooth side of the biscuit to the handle of the spoon. Once the brandy snap is set, slip it off onto a wire rack to cool completely. Continue with the remaining mixture, alternating trays; one tray should be in the oven while you are curling the snaps from the tray before. Keep in an airtight container until ready to fill and serve.

An hour or two before serving, pipe whipped cream into each end of the wafers.

MAKES 24–26

Madeleines

These plump little sponge cakes are baked in special embossed moulds that resemble the 'pleated scallop of the pilgrim's shell', which gives them their characteristic puffed dome. Madeleine pans are available at kitchen and department stores.

2 EGGS
¾ CUP (6 OZ) CASTER (SUPERFINE) SUGAR
½ TEASPOON FINELY GRATED LEMON RIND
1 CUP (4 OZ) PLAIN (ALL-PURPOSE) FLOUR, SIFTED
185 G (6 OZ) BUTTER, CLARIFIED AND COOLED
1 TABLESPOON RUM (OPTIONAL)

Preheat the oven to 200°C (400°F). Butter the madeleine tins (pans) and dust them with flour.

Beat the eggs and sugar together until thick and mousse-like, using a hand whisk and a bowl set over a pan of gently simmering water, or a very good electric mixer. Remove from heat (if using that method) and continue to beat until cooled. Add the lemon rind and fold in the flour and then the clarified butter. Mix only until everything is blended; take care not to overwork the batter at this point, and don't allow the butter to sink to the bottom of the bowl—a metal spoon or spatula is the best tool for this job. Lastly, fold in the rum if using.

Spoon the batter into the madeleine tins. Bake for 8 minutes, until pale golden. Let the cooked madeleines stand for 1–2 minutes before removing them from the tins. Repeat until all the mixture is used.

MAKES 32

To Clarify the Butter. Place the butter in a small saucepan and slowly melt it over a gentle heat. When the butter is clear, remove it from the heat, leave it to stand for a few minutes, and then pour the clear yellow liquid into a cup, leaving the milk sediments in the saucepan. Allow it to cool. This process can also be done in a microwave oven.

Boules de Neige (Snowballs)

Little balls of almond and hazelnut meringue are rolled in snowy white sugar and baked into the most delectable crispy sweet treat. Something quite special to offer as petits fours after dinner. You need sweet paper cases to serve them in.

3 TABLESPOONS EACH GROUND ALMONDS AND
   GROUND HAZELNUTS
¾ CUP (4 OZ) ICING (CONFECTIONERS') SUGAR
1 EGG WHITE
EXTRA ICING SUGAR, FOR DUSTING

Preheat the oven to 160°C (325°F).

Using a mortar and pestle, blender, or food processor, pound the ground nuts together to draw out a little of their oil. Add the sugar gradually and moisten with the egg white, pounding to make a firm paste which can be rolled in the hand.

Divide the mixture into pieces the size of large hazelnuts. Roll each ball in sifted icing sugar in a shallow bowl, to coat thickly. Place them on a baking tray (sheet) lined with baking paper (parchment) and bake until well puffed, about 10 minutes. Cool and transfer to paper cases to serve. Store in an airtight container.

MAKES ABOUT 18

The placement of baking trays (sheets) in the oven is important. Heat should circulate around the trays. During baking, turn the trays sometimes to compensate for uneven baking. If baking one tray at a time, place it in the centre of the oven. If baking two trays, place the oven racks so as to divide the oven into thirds. This allows the heat to circulate and brown the biscuits evenly. If one tray browns quicker than the other, change their positions in the oven during baking. Always preheat the oven.

TARTS AND PASTRIES

The art of pastry making for fruit tarts and other delectable pastries is taught to young people in France with the same seriousness as mathematics. The French consider the greatest compliment one can pay a guest is to offer a homemade pastry.

All good pastries are based on just a few pastry and cake mixtures. It is the combination of these elements and the art of decorating and presenting the pastries that make them so highly prized.

Norman Tart

This tart is made with either pears or apples. The use of Calvados, an apple brandy, is traditional in Normandy.

1 QUANTITY PÂTE SUCRÉE (PAGE 163)
90 G (3 OZ) BUTTER
4 TABLESPOONS CASTER (SUPERFINE) SUGAR
2 EGGS
1 TABLESPOON CALVADOS, KIRSCH OR BRANDY (OPTIONAL)
3 TABLESPOONS PLAIN (ALL-PURPOSE) FLOUR, SIFTED
1 CUP (4 OZ) GROUND ALMONDS
2 LARGE PEARS OR APPLES, JUST RIPE
1 TABLESPOON SUGAR
1 TABLESPOON LEMON JUICE

Wrap the pastry in greaseproof (wax) paper and chill for 1 hour or more before using. Roll the pastry out and use it to line a 23 cm (9 in) flan tin (pie pan) and chill again for 15 minutes. Bake blind (page 160) in a preheated oven at 190°C (375°F) for 8 minutes.

Meanwhile, cream the butter and sugar together and beat in the eggs. Stir in the spirits, if using, and the sifted flour and ground almonds. Spread three-quarters of this mixture into the par-baked tart case (pie shell). Peel the fruit, quarter and cut each quarter into about 4 slices lengthwise. Arrange the slices over the almond cream. Return to the oven and bake for a further 35–40 minutes, sprinkling with the sugar and lemon juice for the last 20 minutes of cooking, until the sugar melts and starts to caramelise.

SERVES 8

Glazed Raspberry Tart

A glorious raspberry tart which is just as lovely made with strawberries. The smallest, reddest strawberries possible should be used.

1 QUANTITY PÂTE SUCRÉE (PAGE 163)
1 QUANTITY CRÈME PÂTISSIÈRE (PAGE 165)
1 PUNNET (250 G/8 OZ) RASPBERRIES
½ CUP (4 FL OZ) REDCURRANT JELLY
1 TABLESPOON WATER
2 TEASPOONS COINTREAU OR 2 TABLESPOONS ORANGE JUICE

Roll out the pastry thinly and use it to line a 23 cm (9 in) flan tin (pie pan). Chill for at least 30 minutes. Prick the base with a fork. Bake blind (page 160) in a preheated oven at 190°C (375°F) for about 20 minutes or until the pastry is a pale biscuit colour. Remove the pastry weights and paper for the last 5 minutes of cooking. Allow to cool.

When cooled, fill with the Crème Pâtissière and spread as evenly as possible. Arrange the raspberries on top, covering the pastry cream completely.

Heat the redcurrant jelly and water in a saucepan, stirring until smooth. Cool slightly, stir in the Cointreau or orange juice. Spoon this glaze over the raspberries and chill.

SERVES 6–8

Overleaf: Two beautiful French tarts. Glazed Raspberry Tart (right) can be made using other berries in season. The Norman Tart (left) has an almond filling which can be made with pears in place of apples.

Flaky Plum Tart

Plums are splendid fruit for tarts. Their sharpness is mellowed by a beautiful buttery pastry.

1 QUANTITY PUFF PASTRY (PAGE 161), CHILLED
500 G (1 LB) PLUMS, HALVED AND STONED (PITTED)
30 G (1 OZ) BUTTER
½ CUP (4 OZ) SUGAR
EGG AND MILK TO GLAZE
EXTRA SUGAR AND ½ TEASPOON GROUND
    CINNAMON, TO FINISH

Preheat the oven to 200°C (400°F). Halve the pastry and roll it out into two rectangles of the same size, each twice as long as it is wide. Lay one half on a wetted baking tray (sheet). Place the plums hollow side down along the pastry on the tray, leaving 1 cm (½ in) around the edges. Dot with butter and sprinkle with sugar. Damp the edges of the pastry.

Fold the second piece of pastry in half. Nick the folded edge at 1 cm (½ in) intervals, leaving 2.5 cm (1 in) at each end uncut. Open the sheet out carefully and lay it on top of the plums, pressing the edges firmly onto those of the lower sheet of pastry.

Brush the top of the tart with beaten egg and milk and sprinkle well with extra sugar and cinnamon. Bake for 30 minutes until golden brown.

Serve hot or warm with cream or ice cream.

SERVES 8

Plum Soufflé Tart

1 QUANTITY PÂTE SUCRÉE (PAGE 163)
3 EGGS, SEPARATED
½ CUP (4 OZ) CASTER (SUPERFINE) SUGAR
3 TABLESPOONS PLAIN (ALL-PURPOSE) FLOUR
1¼ CUPS (10 FL OZ) MILK
1 VANILLA BEAN
6–8 PLUMS, HALVED AND STONED (PITTED)
ICING (CONFECTIONERS') SUGAR, FOR DUSTING

Roll out the pastry and use it to line a 23 cm (9 in) flan tin (pie pan). Trim the edges and chill for 15–30 minutes. Bake blind (page 160) in a preheated oven at 190°C (375°F) for 10 minutes; remove the paper and weights and bake for a further 5 minutes. Remove the pastry from the oven. Increase the temperature to 200°C (400°F).

Beat the egg yolks with the sugar until a ribbon is formed on the mixture when the beaters are lifted. Add the flour and combine. Heat the milk with the vanilla bean in a saucepan. When it comes to the boil, remove the bean and pour the milk over the egg-yolk mixture, beating until well blended. Return to the saucepan and cook gently, stirring until the mixture has thickened. Remove from the heat and keep stirring until the mixture is lukewarm.

Beat the egg whites until stiff. Beat in a little of the custard mixture and gently fold in the rest of it. Pour this into the prepared pastry case (pie shell). Make shallow nests in the filling and spoon in the fruit. (If using canned fruit, drain thoroughly and pat dry with paper towels.)

Bake for 20 minutes, then reduce the temperature to 180°C (350°F) and bake for a further 10–20 minutes or until golden. Cool a little, then dust with sifted icing sugar. Serve warm or at room temperature.

For individual tartlets, try using 8 cm (3½ in) tartlet moulds or egg rings on a baking tray (sheet) to make the pastry cases.

SERVES 8

Muscat Grape Tart

This lovely fresh-cream tart can also be made with blueberries (bilberries) or raspberries in exactly the same way. The pastry is unusual, but it works extremely well with soft fruit tarts such as this.

375 G (12 OZ) MUSCAT GRAPES

2 CUPS (8 OZ) PLAIN (ALL-PURPOSE) FLOUR

½ CUP (4 OZ) CASTER (SUPERFINE) SUGAR

185 G (6 OZ) UNSALTED BUTTER, MELTED AND
    COOLED

A FEW DROPS OF VANILLA ESSENCE (EXTRACT)

1½ CUPS (12 FL OZ) (LIGHT WHIPPING) CREAM, VERY
    COLD, SWEETENED AND FLAVOURED WITH HONEY
    AND VANILLA ESSENCE (EXTRACT) OR ORANGE
    BLOSSOM WATER

Start by carefully peeling and removing the seeds from the grapes. Muscat grapes have the best flavour, but the toughest and most bitter skin (such is life!). As they are also the largest grapes, they don't take long to peel and seed. When they are all done, put them in the refrigerator to chill.

Preheat the oven to 200°C (400°F). Sift the flour into a bowl and stir in the sugar. Add the melted butter and vanilla in a well in the centre and mix all together to make a stiff dough. Press it as you would a crumb crust into a 25 cm (10 in) flan tin (pie pan) with a loose bottom, working up the edges evenly. Prick the base well and bake for about 15–20 minutes until golden and cooked. Remove from the oven and leave to cool completely.

Whip the chilled cream until it holds its shape. When ready to serve, spread the whipped cream in the tart case (shell) and cover with the grapes. Nothing more is needed to decorate the tart. Serve cut into wedges.

SERVES 8–10

Left: Muscat Grape Tart, for which the grapes are peeled, though not completely, so that a little red is left to contrast with the green for a pretty effect.

Right: Walnut Tart, with sweet, skinned walnuts set in a custard filling.

Walnut Tart

1 QUANTITY OF PÂTE SUCRÉE (PAGE 163)

4 EGGS

1 CUP (8 FL OZ) (DOUBLE, LIGHT WHIPPING) CREAM

1 TEASPOON VANILLA ESSENCE (EXTRACT)

125 G (4 OZ) WALNUTS SCALDED, SKINNED AND
    CHOPPED

3 TABLESPOONS LIGHT BROWN SUGAR

3 TABLESPOONS HONEY

Preheat the oven to 190°C (375°F). Roll out the pastry and use it to line a 23 cm (9 in) flan tin (pie pan). Trim the edges, prick the base lightly with a fork and chill for 15 minutes. Bake blind (page 160) for 10 minutes. Remove the beans and paper, turn up the oven to 200°C (400°F) and bake for a further 5–10 minutes until the pastry is lightly coloured and cooked on the bottom. Reduce the oven temperature to 180°C (350°F).

Meanwhile, combine the cream, vanilla, walnuts, brown sugar and honey in a bowl and pour the mixture into the prepared pastry case (pie shell). Bake for 20–30 minutes until the filling is set and pale golden (it will set further on cooling). Serve the tart at room temperature and accompany with a bowl of softly whipped cream.

SERVES 8

Rich Prune and Almond Tart

This is a favourite tart in France, where ripe plums are made into delectable dried prunes, full of rich flavour which the French appreciate. Giant dessert prunes are best, and they don't really need any soaking. I also like to make the tart using soaked dried apricots or nectarines.

1 QUANTITY RICH SHORTCRUST PASTRY (PAGE 161)
    OR PÂTE SUCRÉE (PAGE 163)
125 G (4 OZ) UNSALTED BUTTER
3 TABLESPOONS CASTER (SUPERFINE) SUGAR
2 LARGE EGGS
1 CUP (4 OZ) GROUND ALMONDS
1 TEASPOON VANILLA ESSENCE (EXTRACT)
250 G (8 OZ) PRUNES, PITTED AND SOAKED FOR
    SEVERAL HOURS IN 1 CUP (8 FL OZ) WHITE WINE,
    BRANDY OR TEA
ICING (CONFECTIONERS') SUGAR, FOR DUSTING

Roll out the pastry and use it to line a 23 cm (9 in) round or square flan tin (pie pan); trim the excess. Prick the base with a fork, chill for 15 minutes, then bake blind (page 160) in a preheated oven at 190°C (375°F) for 15 minutes. Remove the paper and beans and cook another 5 minutes. Reduce the oven temperature to 180°C (350°F).

Cream the butter with the sugar until the mixture is light and fluffy, then beat in the eggs one at a time until the mixture is thick and creamy. Beat in the almonds and vanilla essence. Spread the mixture in the prepared flan case (pie shell). Drain the prunes and arrange them on the almond filling. Bake for 40 minutes or until golden. Remove from the oven and dust with sifted icing sugar. Serve warm or at room temperature.

SERVES 8–10

Nectarine Cheese Tart

Nectarines are one of the most luscious stone fruits of the summer season, and this is a delicious French way of using them. Fresh plums or peaches may be used instead of the nectarines. You can also use fresh whole strawberries, raspberries or blueberries (bilberries).

1 QUANTITY PÂTE SUCRÉE (PAGE 163)
250 G (8 OZ) CREAM CHEESE (NEUFCHÂTEL)
4 TABLESPOONS SUGAR
2 EGGS
¼ TEASPOON FRESHLY GRATED NUTMEG OR VANILLA
    ESSENCE (EXTRACT)
5 NECTARINES, STONED (PITTED) AND SLICED
    THICKLY INTO WEDGES
3 TABLESPOONS APRICOT GLAZE (PAGE 169)

Preheat the oven to 190°C (375°F). Roll out the pastry and use it to line a 23 cm (9 in) round or square flan tin (pie pan). Prick the base with a fork, chill for 15 minutes then bake blind (page 160) for 15 minutes. Remove the paper and beans, and return the pastry shell to the oven for a further 10 minutes or until lightly golden. Leave the shell to cool on a rack. Reduce the oven temperature to 180°C (350°F).

Beat the cream cheese with the sugar, then add the eggs, one at a time, beating after each addition. Flavour with the nutmeg or vanilla and beat until the mixture is just smooth. Pour into the shell and bake for 30 minutes. Cool the tart in the tin on a wire rack.

Arrange the nectarine slices in concentric circles on the tart and brush with the warm Apricot Glaze. Allow the glaze to set for at least 5 minutes before serving.

SERVES 8

Parisian Almond Tart

Almonds predominate in this delicious French almond tart, which has good keeping qualities. A fine dusting of icing sugar is its only decoration.

1 QUANTITY RICH SHORTCRUST PASTRY (PAGE 161), USING 1½ CUPS (6 OZ) FLOUR

2 EGG WHITES

1 CUP (8 OZ) SUGAR

2 CUPS (8 OZ) FLAKED OR SLIVERED ALMONDS

¼ TEASPOON GROUND CINNAMON

1 TEASPOON VANILLA ESSENCE (EXTRACT)

ICING (CONFECTIONERS') SUGAR, FOR DUSTING

Preheat the oven to 190°C (375°F). Wrap and chill the pastry for at least 1 hour. Roll it out on a floured board to fit a large flan tin (pie pan) at least 25 cm (10 in) in diameter or two 10 x 25 cm (4 x 10 in) tins. Trim away excess pastry and prick the base lightly with a fork. Chill for a further 15 minutes and then bake blind for 15 minutes (see below). Remove the paper and beans and bake the shell for a further 5 minutes, until pale golden.

Combine the egg whites, sugar, almonds, cinnamon and vanilla in a saucepan; heat, stirring continuously, until the mixture is hot without boiling. Pour the filling into the shell and bake for 20–25 minutes until golden and firm. Dust with icing sugar if liked, and cut the tart into wedges or squares while still warm.

SERVES 8–10

French Cream Cheese Tart

This very simple tart is rich and lovely just as it is, but you may like to serve it with a sharp-sweet fruit such as fresh strawberries or raspberries with a little berry coulis, made by pushing fresh berries through a sieve and sweetening the purée with a little sugar.

1 QUANTITY PÂTE SUCRÉE (PAGE 163), USING 1 CUP (4 OZ) PLAIN (ALL-PURPOSE) FLOUR

125 G (4 OZ) UNSALTED BUTTER, SOFTENED

½ CUP (4 OZ) CASTER (SUPERFINE) SUGAR

250 G (8 OZ) CREAM CHEESE (NEUFCHÂTEL), SOFTENED

½ TEASPOON VANILLA ESSENCE (EXTRACT)

2 EGGS

A PINCH OF GRATED NUTMEG

ICING (CONFECTIONERS') SUGAR, SIFTED, FOR DUSTING

Roll out the pastry to fit a 20 cm (8 in) flan tin (pie pan). Press well into the sides without stretching the pastry. Trim the excess. Prick the base with a fork and chill for a further 15 minutes.

Cream the butter and gradually beat in the sugar. Add the cheese and vanilla, beating well until light and fluffy. Beat the eggs gradually into the cream cheese mixture.

Turn into the uncooked pastry case (pie shell), sprinkle with grated nutmeg and bake in a preheated oven at 190°C (375°F) for 30 minutes, until puffed and golden. Remove from the oven, cool slightly and dust with sifted icing sugar. Serve warm or at room temperature.

SERVES 8

To bake blind: Line the pastry case (pie shell) with baking paper and weigh it down with dried beans or pastry weights. Place in the oven at 190°C (375°F) for 15 minutes or until the pastry is set. Remove the paper and weights. Return the pastry case to the oven for a further 5 minutes. Allow to cool.

Bakewell Tart

A very old English recipe traditionally called Bakewell pudding, it has many variations. This version is close to the one that Lady Shaftesbury made for her husband, a great philanthropist who devoted his life to improving conditions of the East End slums and ragged schools in mid-nineteenth-century London. The mixture is often baked in small tart cases.

1 QUANTITY RICH SHORTCRUST PASTRY (PAGE 161)

60 G (2 OZ) BUTTER

3 TABLESPOONS CASTER (SUPERFINE) SUGAR

1 EGG

4 TABLESPOONS GROUND ALMONDS

A FEW DROPS OF VANILLA OR ALMOND ESSENCE
   (EXTRACT)

RASPBERRY JAM

EXTRA CASTER (SUPERFINE) SUGAR, FOR SPRINKLING

Roll out the pastry and use it to line a 20 cm (8 in) flan tin (pie pan). Chill. Bake blind (page 160) for 10 minutes in a preheated oven at 190°C (375°F). Remove the pastry from the oven and increase the oven temperature to 220°C (425°F).

Meanwhile, cream the butter and gradually beat in the sugar until the mixture is light and fluffy. Beat in the egg, then add the almonds and essence. Beat well.

Spread a layer of jam over the partially baked pastry, then spread the almond mixture on top. Bake for about 30 minutes, until golden brown. Sprinkle with the extra caster sugar.

SERVES 6–8

A Lemon Tart is one of the nicest ways of combining the tartness of lemon with the sweetness of sugar.

Lemon Tart

[handwritten note:] if not wanting cream ⟹ • 3 oeufs • 120 g sucr • 75 g beurre fondu • jus 3 citron

PASTRY

1 CUP (4 OZ) PLAIN (ALL-PURPOSE) FLOUR

3 TABLESPOONS GROUND ALMONDS

75 G (2½ OZ) BUTTER

4 TABLESPOONS ICING (CONFECTIONERS') SUGAR,
   SIFTED

1 EGG YOLK

A FEW DROPS OF VANILLA ESSENCE (EXTRACT)

A PINCH OF SALT

FILLING

4 EGGS

¾ CUP (6 OZ) SUGAR

GRATED RIND AND JUICE OF 2 LEMONS

½ CUP (4 FL OZ) (LIGHT WHIPPING) CREAM

Pastry. Sift the flour with the ground almonds onto a work surface and make a large well in the centre. Put the butter in the well with the icing sugar, egg yolk, vanilla essence and salt, and work these centre ingredients with the fingertips of one hand to a soft paste. Gradually draw in the surrounding flour with a metal spatula and knead lightly to form a dough. Wrap and chill for 1 hour.

Roll out the dough to line a 23 cm (9 in) flan tin (pie pan), pressing the sides in well and trimming the excess. Lightly prick the base and chill for 15 minutes. Bake blind (page 160) in a preheated oven at 200°C (400°F) for 15 minutes, then remove from the oven, lift away the paper and beans, and return to the oven for a further 5 minutes. Reduce the oven temperature to 180°C (350°F).

Filling. Beat the eggs in a bowl with the sugar until smooth. Stir in the lemon rind and juice. Lightly whip the cream and stir into the lemon mixture.

Pour the filling into the prepared pastry case (pie shell) and bake for about 45 minutes. Leave to cool for several hours before serving. Dust if liked with sifted icing sugar.

SERVES 8–10

Treacle Tart

This is an old-fashioned, rich English tart. Traditionally the tart has a full pastry cover or pastry lattice on top, but it can be made without any pastry topping.

1 QUANTITY RICH SHORTCRUST PASTRY (PAGE 161), MADE WITH THE ADDITION OF 1 TEASPOON BAKING POWDER IN THE FLOUR (HALF THE AMOUNT OF BUTTER CAN BE REPLACED BY LARD IF YOU WISH)

4 TABLESPOONS GOLDEN SYRUP (LIGHT TREACLE)

3 TABLESPOONS FRESH WHITE BREADCRUMBS

GRATED RIND OF ½ LEMON AND A GOOD SQUEEZE OF LEMON JUICE

Preheat the oven to 190°C (375°F). Roll out the pastry and use it to line a 20 cm (8 in) pie dish or flan ring (pie pan); trim the excess. Prick with a fork.

Combine the syrup, breadcrumbs, lemon rind and juice in a bowl and spread the mixture in the flan case (pie shell). Roll out the trimmings and leftover pastry, cut into strips and lay them in a lattice pattern on top of the filling. Press down securely around the edges and trim them. Crimp the edges if liked. Press one final strip around the edge. Bake for 35 minutes, until the pastry is cooked and a pleasant brown.

SERVES 6–8

Alternative Filling. Warm the syrup gently and beat in 30 g (1 oz) butter in small pieces, off the heat. When creamy smooth, beat in 2 tablespoons cream, a little grated lemon rind and an egg, beaten lightly. This filling doesn't need a covering, so less pastry is required.

Apple and Mincemeat Tart

2 CUPS (8 OZ) PLAIN (ALL-PURPOSE) FLOUR

A PINCH OF SALT

¼ TEASPOON BAKING POWDER

185 G (6 OZ) UNSALTED BUTTER, CUT INTO SMALL PIECES

2 EGG YOLKS

1–2 TABLESPOONS ICED WATER

A SQUEEZE OF LEMON JUICE

2 CUPS (10 OZ) MINCEMEAT (PAGE 61)

2 APPLES, GRATED

1 EGG WHITE AND SUGAR, FOR GLAZING

Sift the flour, salt and baking powder into a bowl. Rub the butter into the flour until the mixture resembles breadcrumbs. Using a fork, mix the egg yolks with the water and lemon juice, then use a knife to stir this into the flour mixture and form a dough. Knead lightly, wrap and chill for about 1 hour.

Cut away one-quarter of the dough for the lattice top. Roll out the rest and use it to line a 25 cm (10 in) flan tin (pie pan). Trim the edges.

Mix together the mincemeat and grated apple and fill the pastry shell with it. Spread as evenly as possible. Chill. Roll out the remaining pastry and cut it into strips 1 cm (½ in) wide. Weave these pastry strips into a lattice on a piece of baking paper (parchment). Chill. After chilling, shake the lattice top carefully onto the mincemeat filling. Press the edges together firmly and trim. Beat the egg white until just foamy, brush over the pastry top and sprinkle with sugar. Bake in a preheated oven at 190°C (375°F) for 45 minutes until the pastry is golden brown.

Serve warm with whipped cream or vanilla ice cream. Alternatively, flavour softened vanilla ice cream with finely sliced preserved ginger and a little rum, return to the freezer to firm, and serve with the tart.

SERVES 8–10

Little Mince Pies

Mince pies, important for some people to have on hand when friends drop in over Christmas, can be made in advance, frozen and reheated as required. Use small individual tart cases (pie shells), which may vary in size from tiny petit-four pans to two-bite size or slightly larger pans about 5 cm (2 in) in diameter. You can dust the cooled pies with sifted icing (confectioners') sugar or leave them plain. Either way, the taste of the crisp pastry and tangy fruit mincemeat is wonderful.

PASTRY AND FILLING AS FOR APPLE AND MINCEMEAT
   TART (OPPOSITE PAGE)
LIGHTLY BEATEN EGG WHITE, TO GLAZE
2 TABLESPOONS SUGAR

Prepare the pastry and filling as for Apple and Mincemeat Tart. Preheat the oven to 180°C (350°F).

Roll out the pastry and cut half of it into rounds to fit lightly greased patty tins (muffin pans) or small petit-four tins. Moisten edges with the beaten egg and put a teaspoon (more or less) of prepared mincemeat into each.

Cut rounds to fit the tops of the pies. Make a small slit in each pastry lid, or cut out a star using a small star pastry (cookie) cutter. Top each pie with a lid and press the edges firmly to seal. Glaze with beaten egg white and sprinkle well with sugar.

Bake for 20–30 minutes or until golden brown.

MAKES 24 INDIVIDUAL OR 36 PETIT-FOUR SIZE PIES

Mincemeat

A lovely fruit mixture for traditional Christmas pies. Mincemeat matures and improves on keeping, so it can be made several weeks before it is required.

375 G (12 OZ) SEEDLESS RAISINS
250 G (8 OZ) MIXED (CANDIED) PEEL
185 G (6 OZ) SULTANAS (GOLDEN RAISINS)
3 MEDIUM APPLES, PEELED AND CORED
60 G (2 OZ) GLACÉ (CANDIED) CHERRIES
125 G (4 OZ) BLANCHED ALMONDS
100 G (3½ OZ) DRIED APRICOTS
185 G (6 OZ) CURRANTS
2 CUPS (12 OZ) FIRMLY PACKED (LIGHT) BROWN
   SUGAR
GRATED RIND AND JUICE OF 1 LEMON
GRATED RIND OF 1 ORANGE
2 TEASPOONS MIXED SPICE
½ TEASPOON NUTMEG
125–185 G (4–6 OZ) BUTTER, MELTED
4 TABLESPOONS BRANDY OR RUM

Finely chop or mince the raisins, mixed peel, half the sultanas, and the apples, cherries, almonds and apricots. This can be done in a food processor using an on/off action—do not overprocess—and chop fruits separately. Add the remaining sultanas and the currants. Stir in the brown sugar, lemon rind and juice, orange rind, spices, butter and brandy or rum. Mix well and put into a large jar. Cover and chill.

Stir every day for a week, then pack into preserving or jam jars. Cover and store in the refrigerator.

Note: Mixed spice consists of 4 parts cinnamon, 2 parts ground ginger, 1 part ground nutmeg and 1 part ground cloves.

MAKES ABOUT 6 CUPS (30 OZ)

Fruit Tartlets

A tray of glistening fruit tartlets always looks inviting. Choose pretty fluted tart tins (pie pans) or plain ones —you may find oval or little boat shapes. A variety of shapes and fruits is the ultimate offering.

1 QUANTITY PÂTE SUCRÉE (PAGE 163)

GLAZE

1 CUP (12 OZ) JAM (CONSERVE)—APRICOT FOR
   PALE FRUITS AND REDCURRANT JELLY FOR RED
   FRUITS

3 TABLESPOONS WATER

1 TABLESPOON LEMON JUICE

500 G (1 LB) FRESH FRUIT (STRAWBERRIES, APRICOTS,
   PEACHES, PLUMS, GRAPES, PEARS, MANDARINS,
   CHERRIES, RASPBERRIES, BLUEBERRIES (BILBERRIES))

Roll out the pastry thinly and use it to line about 8 tartlet tins (pans). Chill and prick the base of each with a fork. Bake blind (page 160) in a preheated oven at 190°C (375°F) for 8–10 minutes. Allow to cool.

Glaze. Heat all the ingredients over a gentle heat, stirring until smooth. Strain through a sieve. While still warm, brush the inside of the pastry cases (pie shells), leaving the edges clear. This seals the pastry and prevents it from becoming soggy with fruit juice.

Arrange the prepared fruit (see below) in the cases—the fruit should look generous but manageable. Brush the fruit carefully with the glaze until it glistens. Allow to set.

MAKES ABOUT 8

To Prepare Fruits for Tarts. Wash and dry strawberries carefully; hull. They can be left whole if small, sliced or halved.

Poach apricots in a light syrup (½ cup (4 oz) sugar dissolved in 1 cup (8 fl oz) water), until just tender. Drain, remove the stones (pits). Small fruits may be left whole, larger fruits sliced or halved. Good quality preserved fruit may be used.

Prepare peaches and plums in the same way as apricots.

Wash grapes and remove seeds with the pointed end of a small sharp knife.

If using ripe pears, peel them and slice them finely. Sprinkle with a little lemon juice to prevent them from discolouring. If the pears are not quite ripe, peel them and poach them in a light syrup until tender. Drain before slicing.

Peel mandarins and separate into segments. Peel away the outside membrane and dry the segments on paper towels before using.

Wash cherries and remove the stones (pits) with a small sharp knife. Dry before placing them in the tartlet cases.

Raspberries and blueberries (bilberries) can be piled whole into the cases.

Fruit Tartlets with Cream. Prepare the tartlets as above, but cover the bottom of each tart with a little thick cream, mascarpone, or perhaps Créme Patissière (page 165). Arrange fruit on top. Glaze with the melted jam or jelly.

To line plain tartlet tins, roll the pastry out thinly and, using a round cutter, stamp out rounds a little larger than the top of the individual moulds. If using pastry containing sugar or eggs, grease the moulds lightly. Put the pastry rounds into the moulds, pressing lightly to ensure that no air remains between pastry and pan. Prick the shells before baking.

Fresh Fruit Tartlets made with a fabulous selection of succulent fruits in season. The red fruits are brushed with redcurrant glaze, the lighter fruits with apricot glaze.

Apple Galettes

A very rich, crisp pastry circle which holds sliced apples. Use golden delicious apples if possible, to get that very French caramel tinge around the edges. Serve warm or at room temperature with a thick cream if liked.

1½ CUPS (6 OZ) PLAIN (ALL-PURPOSE) FLOUR
A PINCH OF SALT
90 G (3 OZ) UNSALTED BUTTER
3 TABLESPOONS CASTER (SUPERFINE) SUGAR
3 EGG YOLKS
2 DROPS VANILLA ESSENCE (EXTRACT)
750 G–1 KG (1½–2 LBS) DESSERT APPLES
2 TABLESPOONS CASTER (SUPERFINE) SUGAR
15 G (½ OZ) BUTTER
3 TABLESPOONS APPLE JELLY OR APRICOT JAM
   (CONSERVE)
1 TABLESPOON WATER
A SQUEEZE OF LEMON JUICE

Sift the flour with the salt onto a pastry board and make a well in the centre. Place the remaining pastry ingredients in the centre. Work the centre ingredients together with the fingertips of one hand. Using a metal spatula, quickly draw in the flour to form a dough. Knead the pastry lightly until smooth. Wrap and chill for 1 hour or more before using.

Cut the pastry into halves and roll each half into a 20 cm (8 in) circle. Place each circle on a baking tray (sheet) and gently roll a 6 mm (¼ in) edge inwards to form a rim. Prick the base lightly.

Peel the apples and cut into quarters, removing the core. Cut each quarter into thick slices, lengthwise. Arrange the apple slices overlapping to completely cover the pastry rounds. Sprinkle each round with sugar. Top the apple slices with thin slices of butter. Bake the galettes in a preheated oven at 220°C (425°F) for 10–15 minutes or until the edges of the apple are brown and the pastry golden.

Meanwhile, combine the jelly or jam in a pan with the water and lemon juice and bring to the boil, stirring until smooth. Remove the galettes from the oven when cooked and brush with the glaze.

SERVES 6–8

Hot Apple Tarts

A good butter pastry, fragrant apples and thick fresh cream—these make a combination we all enjoy.

1 QUANTITY RICH SHORTCRUST PASTRY (PAGE 161)
6 APPLES SUCH AS GOLDEN DELICIOUS OR GRANNY
   SMITH
APRICOT GLAZE (PAGE 169), WARMED GENTLY

Preheat the oven to 190°C (375°F). Roll out the pastry and cut out 6 rounds the size of bread and butter plates. Arrange three on each baking tray (sheet). Prick the pastry well with a fork.

Peel, halve and core the apples and slice them into thin wedges. Arrange them in overlapping circles over the pastry. Brush the warmed glaze over the apple and bake for 12–15 minutes. Serve warm from the oven and offer plain or with thick fresh cream.

SERVES 6

Pear Tarts

185 G (6 OZ) UNSALTED BUTTER, SOFTENED

½ CUP (4 OZ) SUGAR

2 TEASPOONS VANILLA ESSENCE (EXTRACT)

1 TEASPOON GRATED LEMON RIND

2 TEASPOONS FRESH LEMON JUICE

1 LARGE EGG

1 LARGE EGG YOLK

2½ CUPS (10 OZ) PLAIN (ALL-PURPOSE) FLOUR

1 TEASPOON SALT

½ CUP (5 OZ) APRICOT JAM (CONSERVE)

A SQUEEZE OF LEMON JUICE

6 FIRM RIPE PEARS, PEELED, HALVED AND CORED

CREAM, LIGHTLY WHIPPED, FOR SERVING

Cream the butter with the sugar, and beat in the vanilla, lemon rind and juice. Beat in the egg, then the yolk, until the mixture is smooth. Sift the flour with the salt and fold into the mixture to form a dough. Place on a sheet of plastic wrap (cling film) and pat into a rectangle. Wrap the dough and chill for at least 1 hour.

Unwrap the dough and place it on a floured baking tray (sheet) measuring 45 x 30 cm (18 x 12 in). Dust the dough with a little flour. Roll out the dough to cover the baking tray; trim the edges. Halve the dough lengthwise with a sharp knife, to form two rectangles. Chill for a further 30 minutes.

In a small pan, melt the jam with the lemon juice, then rub through a sieve. Brush some of this glaze over the pastry rectangles, leaving a 20 mm (¾ in) border on the long sides. Cut each halved pear across into thin slices. Arrange the slices, overlapping decoratively, on the glazed part of the pastry. With a spatula, fold the borders of the long sides of the dough up to the edge of the pears and crimp the edges; leave the short ends plain. Sprinkle with sugar.

Bake in a preheated oven at 190°C (375°F) for 30–35 minutes, or until the crust is golden. Remove the tarts from the oven and brush the pears with the remaining apricot glaze. Leave to cool. Serve cut into 12 pieces and offer with the lightly whipped cream.

MAKES 12 SLICES

Nut Rolls

Made with filo (phyllo) pastry, these are a Middle Eastern sweet pastry, extremely easy to make and delightfully light. One type of nut may be used instead of a mixture as in this recipe. The rolls may be served without the syrup and sprinkled with just fine sugar. They keep for 3–4 days. Do not refrigerate.

¾ CUP (3 OZ) FINELY CHOPPED WALNUTS

½ CUP (2 OZ) FINELY CHOPPED ALMONDS

1 TEASPOON SUGAR

¼ TEASPOON CINNAMON

⅛ TEASPOON NUTMEG

10 SHEETS FILO (PHYLLO) PASTRY

250 G (8 OZ) BUTTER, MELTED

CINNAMON HONEY SYRUP

1 CUP (8 OZ) SUGAR

⅔ CUP (6 FL OZ) WATER

3 TABLESPOONS HONEY

1 SMALL CINNAMON STICK

1 TEASPOON FRESH LEMON JUICE

Preheat the oven to 180°C (350°F). Lightly grease a baking tray (sheet). Mix together the nuts, sugar and spices. Stack the filo pastry between two dry tea-towels with a dampened towel on top.

Take 1 sheet of pastry, brush half of it with melted butter, fold the other half over so that you have a piece 18 x 30 cm (7 x 12 in), and brush the top with butter. Sprinkle with 1 tablespoon of nut mixture. Beginning at one end, roll the pastry as you would a jam roll. Cut into three. Place the pastry rolls on a greased baking tray, smooth side up, and brush them with melted butter. Repeat with the remaining pastry and nut filling. Bake for 20 minutes or until golden brown.

Cinnamon Honey Syrup. Mix all the ingredients together and simmer for 30 minutes. Cook only until light brown. Dip the hot nut rolls into the warm syrup or transfer the rolls to a flat dish with sides and pour over the hot strained syrup. Leave until cool. Drain on a wire cake rack set over a tray.

MAKES 30

Pithiviers

This is the traditional cake served on Twelfth Night in France. It can be baked in a round or oblong, and is easy to make now that frozen puff pastry sheets are available—you can, of course, make your own puff pastry (page 161). This cake is delicious served warm.

90 G (3 OZ) UNSALTED BUTTER

3 TABLESPOONS CASTER (SUPERFINE) SUGAR

1 EGG YOLK

100 G (3½ OZ) GROUND ALMONDS

1 TABLESPOON RUM

1 SHEET READY-ROLLED PUFF PASTRY, THAWED

1 EGG, BEATEN, FOR GLAZE

2 TABLESPOONS SUGAR

Cream the butter and caster sugar. Beat in the egg yolk, ground almonds and rum.

Cut the pastry sheet into halves. Place one half on a buttered baking tray (sheet), fill the centre with the almond filling, flattening it out, but leave the edges clear. Top with the remaining pastry and press the edges together. With a sharp knife cut the top of the pastry (but not through) in a decorative pattern, swirls or herringbone. Chill until ready to bake. Brush with beaten egg glaze.

Bake in a preheated oven at 200°C (400°F) for 15 minutes, then reduce the temperature to 180°C (350°F) and bake for another 10 minutes. Sprinkle with the sugar and return to the oven for a further 5–10 minutes to give the pastry a crisp, caramelised glaze. Serve warm with coffee or with whipped cream as a dessert.

SERVES 6

Pithiviers can be made round or rectangular. Puff pastry sheets are filled with a mixture of ground almonds, eggs and sugar, often flavoured with rum.

Jalousie

One of the most famous French pastries: rectangles of flaky pastry enclosing sweet cooked fruit, such as apples or apricots, or perhaps raspberry or strawberry conserve. The top layer of pastry is decorated with fine cuts which give a French shutter effect, hence the name 'jalousie'. Serve sliced with whipped cream.

2 SHEETS READY-ROLLED PUFF PASTRY OR

    1 QUANTITY HOMEMADE PUFF PASTRY (PAGE 161)

2–3 APPLES, PEELED, CORED AND SLICED

30 G (1 OZ) BUTTER

2 TABLESPOONS SUGAR

2 TABLESPOONS SULTANAS (GOLDEN RAISINS)

1 TABLESPOON RUM

1 EGG, BEATEN, FOR GLAZING

Thaw the pastry if using frozen sheets, or have your homemade puff pastry chilled. To make the filling, cook the apples in the butter until soft and golden, add the sugar, sultanas and rum. Heat gently, then allow to cool.

Cut each ready-rolled pastry sheet in half. Alternatively, divide the homemade pastry in two, roll each piece into a rectangle about 20 x 30 cm (8 x 12 in) and cut these in half to make four 20 x 15 cm (8 x 6 in) rectangles.

Place one rectangle of pastry on a greased baking tray (sheet) and spread the centre with the cooked apple, leaving the edges clear. Paint the edges with the beaten egg. Make cuts about 20 mm (¾ in) apart across a second piece of pastry, leaving a border of uncut pastry all round. Place the cut pastry on top of the base, pressing the edges firmly together. Brush the top with egg glaze.

Repeat with the other two pastry strips and apple filling.

Bake in a preheated oven at 200°C (400°F) for 30 minutes until the pastry is golden and well risen. Serve sliced with whipped cream.

SERVES 10–12

Eccles Cakes

These little cakes, really pastries, are among my favourites. As a shortcut you can use commercial or flaky pastry; otherwise use your own puff pastry.

2 CUPS (8 OZ) PLAIN (ALL-PURPOSE) FLOUR
½ TEASPOON SALT
125 G (4 OZ) FIRM BUTTER, CUT INTO SMALL PIECES
ABOUT 4 TABLESPOONS ICED WATER
1 EGG WHITE, SLIGHTLY BEATEN
CASTER (SUPERFINE) SUGAR, FOR DUSTING
FILLING
½ CUP (3 OZ) FINELY CHOPPED MIXED (CANDIED)
    PEEL (OPTIONAL)
½ TEASPOON EACH GROUND ALLSPICE AND NUTMEG
1½ CUPS (7 OZ) CURRANTS
45 G (1½ OZ) BUTTER
4 TABLESPOONS SUGAR

Sift the flour and salt into a bowl. Rub in the butter until the mixture resembles bread-crumbs. Make a well in the centre and add enough of the water to make a firm pastry dough. Do not knead. Form into a ball, wrap and chill for 1 hour.

Grease baking trays (sheets) and preheat the oven to 200°C (400°F).

Roll out the pastry on a lightly floured surface. Using a saucer or 6–8 cm (2½–3 in) cutter, cut out rounds of pastry. (You will need to re-roll the scraps of pastry to get approximately 8.) Place a rounded teaspoon of filling (see below) in the centre of each round. Gather up the edges into the centre and pinch them together. Turn the cake over and flatten it slightly with rolling pin. Make three small slits in the top, brush with the egg white and sprinkle with caster sugar. Place on the prepared trays and bake for 15–20 minutes or until pale golden.

Filling. Place all ingredients in a saucepan and heat gently until the butter melts. Put in a bowl and allow to cool.

MAKES 8

Millefeuilles

'A thousand leaves', as the name of this confection translates from the French, refers to the many flaky layers of puff pastry, layered alternately with cream. The filling often includes a raspberry or strawberry jam. Here fresh berries are used, both to fill the pastry and to make an accompanying coulis sauce. Instead of one large, three-layered oblong millefeuilles, I like to make individual round ones.

1 QUANTITY PUFF PASTRY (PAGE 161) OR
    185 G (6 OZ) COMMERCIAL PUFF PASTRY, THAWED
1–2 PUNNETS (250–500 G/8 OZ–1 LB)
    STRAWBERRIES, HULLED
1 PUNNET (250 G/8 OZ) RASPBERRIES
ICING (CONFECTIONERS') SUGAR
A SQUEEZE OF LEMON JUICE
1 CUP (8 FL OZ) (DOUBLE) CREAM, FOR WHIPPING
VANILLA ESSENCE (EXTRACT)

Roll out the pastry to 3 mm (⅛ in) thickness, dusting the surface and rolling pin with icing sugar in place of flour. Cut into four 9 cm (3½ in) rounds. Place on a baking tray (sheet) rinsed in cold water; alternatively, cut into oblongs each the same size. Place the trimmings on the tray as well. Chill for 15 minutes, then bake in a preheated oven at 220°C (425°F) for about 10 minutes until golden, risen and flaky. Remove from the oven.

The pastry rounds should split in half to make eight rounds. Hollow out the centre inside of each with a sharp-pointed knife. Return to the oven for a few minutes to thoroughly cook the centres. Again, save any trimmings, cooking further if necessary. Remove to a rack to cool.

Meanwhile, purée half the strawberries in a blender with the raspberries, adding icing sugar and lemon juice to taste to make a coulis. Quarter the remaining strawberries and stir through half the coulis. Whip the cream in a well-chilled bowl, adding vanilla essence and icing sugar to taste, until almost stiff.

To assemble, spread a little whipped cream over each of four pastry circles, making sure to fill the cavity, then top with some of the strawberry and coulis mixture. Carefully spoon or pipe a little cream over the fruit and place the remaining pastry circles, cavity side down, on top. Dust the sides with some of the crushed pastry trimmings. Arrange on serving plates. Pour the coulis around each one and dust with icing sugar.

MAKES 4

Mint Cakes

These delicious little cakes have an intriguing flavour. They are easy to make with commercial puff pastry.

½ CUP (3 OZ) MIXED (CANDIED) PEEL
1½ TABLESPOONS SUGAR
2 TABLESPOONS FINELY CHOPPED MINT
30 G (1 OZ) BUTTER
2 SHEETS READY-ROLLED PUFF PASTRY
EGG WHITE, LIGHTLY BEATEN
CASTER (SUPERFINE) SUGAR

Preheat the oven to 200°C (400°F). Lightly grease a baking tray (sheet).

Combine the peel, sugar, mint and butter in a bowl and mix well. Cut 10 cm (4 in) rounds from the pastry. Place teaspoons of the filling in the centre of each round, dampen the edges of the pastry and draw them together to enclose the filling, making a round or oval shape. Turn smooth side up, cut three slits to expose the filling, then flatten slightly with a rolling pin, so the filling just shows through.

Place on the prepared baking tray (sheet), brush with egg white and sprinkle with caster sugar. Bake for 10–15 minutes or until the pastry is golden brown and crisp.

MAKES 8

Palmiers

These popular French pastries get their name from the French word for the date palm, which they resemble after being rolled, sliced and pressed out. The sprinkling of sugar caramelises during the baking, giving the pastries a lovely golden glow.

1 SHEET READY-ROLLED PUFF PASTRY
½ CUP (4 OZ) SUGAR

Preheat the oven to 220°C (425°F).

Brush the pastry with water and sprinkle with sugar. Fold in three and roll again to a square about the original size, using sugar, not flour, to prevent the pastry sticking to the board. Fold one side twice to the centre, then fold the opposite side in the same manner, taking care that the folds meet in the centre. Now turn one fold on to the other and press firmly.

Cut into pieces across the folds about 12 mm (½ in) thick and place on a damp baking tray (sheet) cut side down and fairly well apart. Press each with heel of the hand to flatten.

Bake for 8 minutes; when the underside is well caramelised, turn the palmiers over and bake for a further 3–4 minutes. They can be served plain or sandwiched with whipped cream.

MAKES ABOUT 20

Pastry should be chilled for at least 30 minutes before it is rolled out. This allows it to relax and lose its elasticity. After rolling the pastry and lining the tin or pan with it, chill again.

DRINKS

The tinkle of ice on fine crystal, the clink of a silver stirrer in the goblet—gentle ways of announcing that something special is coming up, something to restore sweetness to the soul.

There's nothing quite like the simple joy of mixing a planter's mint julep on a summer's day, offering a favourite aunt a refreshing lemon barley water, or blending a Mexican coffee on a cold wintry day.

Thirst Quenchers

Clear sunny days, brilliant blue skies and high temperatures which linger on into the evening make us yearn for something cool. A long iced lemonade or a sweet fragrant rose-water; lassi, a yogurt drink much appreciated in hot, hot India; pretty-as-a-picture fruit frosts—all are perfect for summertime sipping.

Ginger Beer

Homemade ginger beer is easy to make and is a most refreshing drink.

GINGER BEER PLANT
6 SULTANAS
JUICE OF 1 LEMON
2 TEASPOONS SUGAR
1 TEASPOON GROUND GINGER
½ TEASPOON LEMON PULP
⅔ CUP (¼ IMP. PT) COLD WATER
FEEDING
4 TEASPOONS SUGAR
2 TEASPOONS GROUND GINGER
JUICE OF 1 LEMON
GINGER BEER
1 CUP (8 OZ) SUGAR
1¼ CUPS (10 FL OZ) BOILING WATER
1.5 LITRES (2¾ IMP. PT) COLD WATER

Ginger Beer Plant. Put all the ingredients in a screw-topped jar and leave for 3 days. In warm weather the mixture should start to ferment after this time; it may take a little longer in cooler weather.
Feeding. On each of the next 4 days add 1 teaspoon sugar and ½ teaspoon ground ginger. On the following day, strain into a bowl through two thicknesses of fine muslin (cheesecloth) and add the juice of 1 lemon to the resulting liquid.
Ginger Beer. Dissolve the sugar in the boiling water, then add the cold water. Mix this into the strained ginger beer plant. Pour into 3 sterilised screw-topped bottles or jars. The ginger beer will be ready to drink after about 3 weeks. It is important to store the bottles in a cool, dark place.

Note: If a continuous supply is wanted, double the ingredients for the plant and also double the daily feed. After straining, retain half the sediment, add ⅔ cup (6 fl oz) of cold water and continue to feed as above.

MAKES ABOUT 3 BOTTLES

Iced Plantation Tea

Non-alcoholic and most refreshing on a hot summery day. Use a black tea like Darjeeling or orange pekoe.

3 TABLESPOONS TEA LEAVES
3 CUPS (24 FL OZ) BOILING WATER
6 HANDFULS MINT SPRIGS
¾ CUP (6 OZ) SUGAR
2.5 LITRES (4 IMP. PTS) BOILING WATER
1 CUP (8 FL OZ) LEMON JUICE
MINT SPRIGS, TO GARNISH

Place the tea leaves in a large enamelled saucepan and pour on the 3 cups of boiling water. Swirl around to 'dust' the tea, then pour off the water, leaving the tea leaves still in the pan. Add the mint and sugar to the pan and pour on the 2.5 litres of boiling water. Cover and leave to infuse for about 15 minutes. Strain and add the lemon juice. Pour over ice in chilled glasses, garnishing each with a mint sprig.

MAKES AT LEAST 10–12 DRINKS

Grape Zip

2 CUPS (16 FL OZ) GRAPE JUICE
CRUSHED ICE
DRY GINGER ALE
THIN SLICES OF LEMON OR LIME

Pour the grape juice into 4 small glasses and fill with crushed ice and dry ginger ale. Mix and top each with a lemon slice.

SERVES 4

Overleaf: Rose-Water Cordial is poured over crushed ice and finished with pomegranate seeds to make a non-alcoholic thirst-quencher. Alongside are two glasses of Mai Tai, from Hawaii, a drink based on pineapple juice and rum.

Apple Blossom Cooler

So pretty and inviting, especially on a hot day.

4 TABLESPOONS SUGAR
1 CUP (8 FL OZ) WATER
A FEW LARGE MINT SPRIGS
1 CINNAMON STICK
1.25 LITRES (2 IMP. PTS) APPLE JUICE
½ CUP (4 FL OZ) STRAINED LEMON JUICE
FLOWERS AND MINT SPRIGS, TO GARNISH

Dissolve the sugar in the water with the mint and cinnamon over gentle heat and bring to the boil. Simmer about 10 minutes, then cool and strain. Combine with the apple and lemon juices, strain into a large jug and fill with ice cubes. Garnish with small flowers from the garden and mint sprigs.

SERVES 6

Lemonade

Old-fashioned lemonade is still one of the loveliest summer drinks for all ages.

WATER
SUGAR
LEMON JUICE

For each cup of water, use 3–4 tablespoons of sugar and 1½ tablespoons of lemon juice.

Make a syrup first: dissolve the sugar in the water over a gentle heat and let it come to the boil; boil for 2 minutes. Chill this syrup and add the measured lemon juice. Keep the lemon syrup in bottles in the refrigerator until needed.

Plenty of ice and chilled water can be used to dilute the syrup and make a lemonade to taste. It can also be made sparkling with the addition of mineral water or soda water.

Lemon Barley Water

This refreshing drink, very popular in Victorian times, is enjoying a revival today. It keeps well in the refrigerator.

3–4 TABLESPOONS PEARL BARLEY
4 CUPS (1½ IMP. PTS) WATER
THINLY PEELED RIND AND JUICE OF 2 LEMONS
SUGAR TO TASTE

Place the barley, water and lemon rind in a saucepan and bring to the boil. Lower the heat and simmer as gently as possible, covered, for 2 hours. Strain into a container and add the lemon juice and sugar to taste, about 3–4 tablespoons. Stir well to dissolve the sugar. Cool, then chill. Dilute with chilled water to taste.

MAKES ABOUT 6 DRINKS

Lassi

There are several versions of this cooling Indian yoghurt drink. Some are salty, sometimes with a gentle spicing of cumin; others are like this one, sweetened, with or without the fragrance of rose-water. It is important that the yoghurt is rich and creamy. If it isn't, add the cream. For a longer, cooler and very refreshing drink, replace half the yoghurt with soda water.

3 CUPS NATURAL (PLAIN) YOGURT
½ CUP (4 OZ) SUGAR
3 TABLESPOONS DOUBLE CREAM (OPTIONAL)
1 TABLESPOON ROSE-WATER
ABOUT 8 ICE CUBES

Mix the yoghurt, sugar, cream and rose-water in a blender. Blend quickly, adding the ice cubes one at a time until smooth and frothy. Pour into glasses and serve.

SERVES 2–3

Ginger Julep

The idea of tender mint sprigs chopped with sugar and lemon—the refreshing flavour impregnating the sugar comes from Kentucky. This non-alcoholic version is refreshing, without the impact of bourbon.

A BUNCH OF MINT
¾ CUP (6 OZ) CASTER (SUPERFINE) SUGAR
1 CUP (8 FL OZ) STRAINED LEMON JUICE
3 LARGE BOTTLES DRY GINGER ALE, WELL CHILLED
1 LEMON, THINLY SLICED

Remove the leaves from the mint stalks and chop finely in an electric blender or food processor with the sugar and lemon juice. Scoop the mixture into a jug, cover and leave to stand for 2 hours, stirring occasionally. When ready to serve, half-fill a tall jug with ice cubes and strain or pour unstrained a third of the mint mixture on top. Fill up the jug with one of the bottles of dry ginger ale, stir and decorate with thin slices of lemon. Repeat with the remaining ingredients once the jug has been emptied. This quantity makes plenty for a non-alcoholic party drink.

When preparing ice for sparkling, fresh-tasting drinks, use ice that has been isolated from foods in the refrigerator; ice quickly absorbs undesirable odours.
To rid ice of these odours, rinse it quickly under cold water.
To obtain the cracked or crushed ice called for in certain recipes, use one of the several manual or electric ice crushers on the market, or a food processor equipped for the purpose, doing just a few cubes at the time. Or simply wrap the cubes in a strong tea towel or double thickness of plastic wrapping and break them up with a hammer.

Ginger Julep combines mint, sugar and lemon, which is poured over dry ginger ale and ice.

Rose-Water Cordial

Cooking with rose-water is an ancient art in the Middle East, where roses are grown commercially for their oil. Rose flavouring is used in sweets, cakes, pastries, jams and puddings, even in main dishes. This wonderfully cooling drink makes a welcome change from alcoholic drinks during the heat of summer.

2 CUPS (1 LB) SUGAR
1¼ CUPS (10 FL OZ) WATER
1 TABLESPOON LEMON JUICE
RED FOOD COLOURING
3 TABLESPOONS ROSE-WATER
POMEGRANATE SEEDS, TO DECORATE (IF AVAILABLE)

In a heavy saucepan, dissolve the sugar in the water over a gentle heat. Add the lemon juice and simmer for about 5 minutes. Add the colouring and stir well. Stir in the rose-water and simmer for a few minutes longer. Cool and store in a clean, dry bottle.

To serve, dilute to taste with ice-cold water, soda water or sparkling mineral water, finishing each glass with a few pomegranate seeds if available.

MAKES ABOUT 20 DRINKS

Iced Spiced Cider

This very refreshing punch varies with the alcoholic content of the cider. For an alcoholic lift, add a measure of maraschino liqueur or brandy to taste.

3 LITRES (5 IMP. PTS) APPLE CIDER
2 TABLESPOONS WHOLE CLOVES
8 CINNAMON STICKS
MINT SPRIGS, TO GARNISH

Put the cider, cloves and cinnamon in a large enamelled saucepan and bring to the boil. Remove from the heat. Cover and leave to cool and infuse for at least 1 hour. Strain into a glass jug and chill thoroughly. Add a sprig of mint to each glass.

MAKES 12–18 DRINKS

Cups, Cordials and Drinks with a Dash

Sharing a drink is a universal symbol of friendship, particularly when there is something to celebrate— a birthday, an anniversary, Christmas, a wedding, times when we want to drink a toast of well-wishing. Let me provide you with a little support for those occasions with recipes to match the effervescence of the occasion.

Orange Blossoms

Use a glass punchbowl for this cocktail.

1 CUP (8 FL OZ) GIN
4 TABLESPOONS APRICOT BRANDY, WELL CHILLED
4 CUPS (1½ IMP. PTS) ORANGE JUICE, WELL CHILLED
½ CUP (4 FL OZ) LEMON JUICE, CHILLED

Mix everything together in a punch bowl and serve in cocktail or wide champagne glasses taken from a bucket of ice.

MAKES 6–8 DRINKS

Pineapple Fizz

Fizzes have always been popular in America. Try spiking this with rum! If you want a longer, cooler drink, fill up the glass with sparkling soda water.

2 CUPS (16 FL OZ) PINEAPPLE JUICE
1 EGG WHITE
4 ICE CUBES
2 TABLESPOONS RUM (OPTIONAL)
SMALL SPEARS OF FRESH PINEAPPLE OR MINT SPRIGS,
    TO GARNISH

Blend all the ingredients (except the garnish) together until frothy using an electric blender or shake in a cocktail shaker. Pour into 2 tall glasses, garnish with pineapple spears or mint.

SERVES 2

Pineapple and Orange Cooler

Rum leads us to thoughts of Jamaica or Queensland, sugar plantations, pineapples and other tropical delights. Try this rum cooler on a warm day and dream you're in the Havana Club!

1 CUP (8 FL OZ) FRESH PINEAPPLE CUBES
1 CUP (8 FL OZ) STRAINED ORANGE JUICE
3 TABLESPOONS RUM
2 TABLESPOONS HONEY
2 TABLESPOONS LIME OR LEMON JUICE
ICE
POMEGRANATE SEEDS, TO GARNISH (OPTIONAL)

Blend all the ingredients (except the pomegranate seeds) together in a blender, pour into 2 tall glasses and fill with ice cubes. Scoop in some pomegranate seeds to garnish.

SERVES 2

Blackcurrant Spritz

This is the perfect refresher on a warm evening. It looks so pretty and inviting.

4 TABLESPOONS CRÈME DE CASSIS
1 CUP (8 FL OZ) APPLE JUICE, CHILLED
1 CUP (8 FL OZ) ROSÉ WINE OR FRUITY WHITE WINE,
    CHILLED
SODA WATER

Pour the crème de cassis into 6–8 fluted glasses half-filled with ice cubes. Combine the apple juice and wine, and stir well to mix. Divide between the glasses. Top each glass with soda water.

SERVES 6–8

Kir and Kir Royal

The blackcurrant liqueur crème de cassis is rather expensive, but for very special friends or a festive occasion, why not splash out and buy a bottle. It goes a long way mixed with champagne (no need to use a costly one) for Kir Royal, or a crisp white wine such as chablis for Kir. Either way, a great cooling drink.

½ CUP (4 FL OZ) CRÈME DE CASSIS
1 BOTTLE CHAMPAGNE OR CHABLIS, WELL CHILLED

Have champagne glasses well chilled and the champagne or still wine on ice. Pour a little crème de cassis into each glass and top with the wine. Stir and drink.

MAKES 6–8 DRINKS

Frozen Daiquiris

Daiquiri is a great summer drink and one of the great cocktails. It was created in Havana and made famous with the help of Ernest Hemingway. This version is frozen into a mush like granita, which quickly turns into an icy drink.

3 PARTS WHITE RUM
1 PART LIME OR LEMON JUICE
3 PARTS WATER
A LITTLE SUGAR (JUST TO TASTE)
MINT SPRIGS AND THIN LIME SLICES, TO GARNISH

Mix the rum, citrus juice, water and sugar to taste in a large jug, cover, and freeze overnight. Remove from the freezer about 30 minutes before serving and scoop into cocktail glasses. Garnish with mint and thin lime slices.

Cider Cup

Select a pretty bowl, fill it with this lovely fruity cup and set it on a tray decorated with fresh garden leaves, with punch or wine glasses, ready to welcome guests.

½ CUP (4 FL OZ) MARASCHINO LIQUEUR OR KIRSCH
½ CUP (4 FL OZ) ORANGE CURAÇAO
½ CUP (4 FL OZ) BRANDY
1.25 LITRES (2 IMP. PTS) DRY CIDER, WELL CHILLED

Pour everything into a large glass bowl or jug. Add ice and stir gently. Float a few strawberries or orange slices on top, if liked.

MAKES 8–10 DRINKS

Iced Tea Punch

Here's a punch for a large group of friends. It's not as sweet as some you may encounter, which makes it a little more sophisticated. A punchbowl or large glass jug is called for.

1.25 LITRES (2 IMP. PTS) BOILING WATER
3 TABLESPOONS TEA LEAVES
3½ CUPS (28 FL OZ) WHITE WINE, CHILLED
½ CUP (4 FL OZ) LEMON JUICE
CRUSHED ICE
WHOLE STRAWBERRIES OR CHERRIES
PIECES OF FRESH PINEAPPLE
A FEW SLICES OF LEMON OR ORANGE
CASTER (SUPERFINE) SUGAR, TO TASTE

Pour the boiling water over the tea leaves and leave to infuse for 5 minutes. Strain into a bowl. Cool. Add the wine and lemon juice. Pour into a punchbowl or large pretty glass jug with crushed ice. Garnish with fruit. Sweeten with sugar.

SERVES 10–12

Mint Juleps

Southern hospitality often begins with a deliciously cooling mint julep. They are moreish, but be warned: they can be dangerous!

¾ CUP (6 OZ) SUGAR
1½ CUPS (12 FL OZ) WATER
24 SPRIGS OF FRESH YOUNG MINT LEAVES
CRUSHED ICE
2½ CUPS (1 IMP. PT) BOURBON OR WHISKY
FRESH STRAWBERRIES, IF LIKED

Make a syrup by dissolving the sugar in the water over a gentle heat. Bruise half of the mint leaves and add them to the sugar syrup. Simmer over a gentle heat for about 20 minutes. Cool, strain and chill.

Fill tall glasses or large brandy balloons with crushed ice and a generous sprig of mint. Pour julep mixture halfway up the glass and pour in a good nip of bourbon or whisky. Decorate the top of each glass with a strawberry. Put in a couple of drinking straws and serve.

SERVES 6–8

Pawpaw and Watermelon Frosts

A wonderfully refreshing cocktail which can be made non-alcoholic by simply leaving out the rum.

1 CUP (8 FL OZ) DICED PAWPAW (PAPAYA)
1 CUP (8 FL OZ) DICED WATERMELON, FROZEN
½ CUP (4 FL OZ) ORANGE JUICE
1 CUP (8 FL OZ) CRUSHED ICE
ORANGE SLICES AND MINT SPRIGS, TO GARNISH
2 TABLESPOONS WHITE RUM

In a blender or liquidiser, purée the pawpaw with the watermelon, orange juice and ice until smooth but still frosty. Pour into two tall glasses and garnish with orange slices and mint sprigs. Float a tablespoon of rum over each.

MAKES 2 DRINKS

Honeydew Rum Freezes

3 CUPS (24 FL OZ) DICED HONEYDEW MELON, FROZEN
¾ CUP (6 FL OZ) RUM
2 TABLESPOONS MIDORI (MELON-FLAVOURED LIQUEUR) (OPTIONAL)
1 TABLESPOON FRESH LIME OR LEMON JUICE
4 THIN LIME SLICES

Purée the honeydew with the rum, liqueur and juice, scraping down the sides once or twice, until the mixture is smooth and still frozen. Pour into 4 stemmed glasses and decorate each with a lime slice.

MAKES 4 DRINKS

Ramoz Fizz

A fizz is a long, sparkling drink, ideal for summer.

2 TABLESPOONS GIN OR VODKA
2 TABLESPOONS LEMON JUICE
1 TABLESPOON ORANGE JUICE
1 TEASPOON ORANGE FLOWER WATER
1 EGG WHITE
1 TABLESPOON THICK CREAM
1 TEASPOON SUGAR
½ CUP (4 FL OZ) CRACKED ICE
SODA WATER, TO TOP UP
LEMON JUICE AND CASTER (SUPERFINE) SUGAR FOR GLASS

Mix the liquor, juices, flower water, egg white, cream, sugar and ice together in a blender, or shake vigorously in a cocktail shaker, until the mixture is smooth and frothy. Pour into a tall tumbler that has been dipped in a little lemon juice then into caster sugar. Fill three-quarters full and top with soda water.

MAKES 1 GREAT DRINK

By whizzing frozen fruits in a blender, wonderfully refreshing summer drinks such as Paw Paw and Watermelon Frosts and Honeydew Rum Freezes can be made simply.

Mai Tai

From Hawaii and as pretty as a picture.

2 TABLESPOONS LIGHT RUM
½ CUP (4 FL OZ) UNSWEETENED PINEAPPLE JUICE
½ CUP (4 FL OZ) ORANGE JUICE
½ CUP (4 FL OZ) LEMON JUICE
A GOOD DASH OF GRAND MARNIER
CRUSHED ICE
DARK RUM
PINEAPPLE SPEARS, SLIVERS OF LIME OR ORANGE
 RIND AND FRESH MINT LEAVES, TO GARNISH

Shake or blend together the light rum, juices
and Grand Marnier. Pour into tall glasses over
crushed ice. Float some dark rum on top of
each drink. Decorate with pineapple spears,
lime or orange rind, and mint slipped onto
toothpicks (cocktail sticks). Serve with straws.

SERVES 2

Orange Vodka Cocktail

*Vodka may be strong and rather tasteless by itself,
but when mixed with orange juice it makes a delicious,
smooth cocktail. Crack the ice in a blender or use an
ice crusher.*

1 CUP (8 FL OZ) CRACKED ICE
½ CUP (4 FL OZ) ORANGE JUICE
1½ TABLESPOONS VODKA
1 TABLESPOON ORANGE CURAÇAO (OR COINTREAU
 OR GRAND MARNIER)
1 TABLESPOON LEMON JUICE
1 TABLESPOON CASTER (SUPERFINE) SUGAR
1 THIN SLICE OF ORANGE OR SPIRAL OF ORANGE
 RIND, TO GARNISH

Mix the ice with the orange juice, vodka,
curaçao, lemon juice and sugar in a blender
or cocktail shaker. Pour into a tall chilled
glass and garnish with the orange slice or
spiral.

MAKES 1 DRINK

Warm-Ups

*A hot, spirited drink is a cheerful way of combating a
nippy winter's day—something to brace you against
the chilly air.*

*After a day in the mountains, what could be better
than a hot eggnog? Perhaps you prefer a rich and
creamy Mexican coffee, or the ultimate in high drama,
café brûlot, sweet, spicy and flaming. Winter has its
rewards.*

*And for those who dine late, mint tea—a light herb
tisane—is just the thing as a digestive.*

Mexican Coffee

*Chocolate was first used as a hot drink, and Mexicans
are expert at mixing it.*

30 G (1 OZ) DARK (SEMI-SWEET) CHOCOLATE
1 CUP (8 FL OZ) MILK
SUGAR TO TASTE
2 DROPS BITTER ALMOND ESSENCE (EXTRACT)
¼ TEASPOON GROUND CINNAMON
3 TABLESPOONS COGNAC OR BRANDY
1 CUP (8 FL OZ) COFFEE, HOT AND STRONG

Melt the chocolate in the top of a double
boiler over a gentle heat. Scald the milk in
another saucepan, then add it to the melted
chocolate, a little at a time, whisking with a
rotary whisk. Pour the mixture back into the
milk pan, adding the sugar, almond essence,
cinnamon and brandy, and heat gently, still
whisking, until smooth and frothy.

Half-fill 2 glass mugs or 3 cups with the
chocolate mixture and top up each to fill with
the hot coffee.

MAKES 2–3

Mint Tea

Increasingly, those who dine late prefer to drink a tisane—herb tea—rather than coffee. Mint tea taken hot after a meal acts as a marvellous digestive.

4 LARGE FRESH MINT SPRIGS OR 2 TEASPOONS DRIED
    MINT LEAVES
BOILING WATER
SUGAR IF DESIRED

Put the fresh or dried mint in a heatproof jug or clean teapot. Pour on the boiling water, stir and allow to infuse for 3–5 minutes. Strain into cups or heatproof glasses and serve. Sweeten to taste with sugar.

Café Brûlot

Brûlot sets of bowls, ladles and cups are a traditional wedding gift in New Orleans. Café Brûlot can also be made in a chafing dish at the table and served in demitasse cups.

¾ CUP (6 FL OZ) BRANDY
4 WHOLE CLOVES
1 CINNAMON STICK
4 STRIPS THINLY PARED ORANGE RIND
6 SUGAR LUMPS
A 6-CUP POT OF STRONG BLACK COFFEE

In a small saucepan heat the brandy, flavourings and sugar. When the sugar has dissolved, remove the pan from the heat and place it on a serving tray with the cups and coffee pot.

Flame the brandy mixture, then pour some into each cup. Fill them up with coffee, provide your guests each with a coffee spoon to stir, and serve.

MAKES 6 CUPS

Hot Chocolate

Spanish hot chocolate is incredibly rich, a special treat to give comfort on cold mornings or nights. Best made with dark chocolate.

125 G (4 OZ) DARK (SEMI-SWEET) CHOCOLATE
2½ CUPS (1 IMP. PT) MILK

Melt the chocolate in the top of a double boiler over a gentle heat. Scald the milk in another saucepan, then add it to the melted chocolate, a little at a time, whisking with a rotary whisk. Pour the mixture back into the milk pan and heat gently, still whisking, until smooth and frothy. Serve as soon as possible.

MAKES 2 MUGS OR 4 SMALL CUPS

Hot Eggnog

A wonderful restorative drink, traditional at Christmas time in the United States. Children will enjoy eggnog without the rum.

2 EGGS
2 TABLESPOONS HONEY
A PINCH OF SALT
1½ CUPS (12 FL OZ) MILK, SCALDED AND HOT
1–2 TABLESPOONS RUM OR 1 TEASPOON VANILLA
    ESSENCE (EXTRACT) (OPTIONAL)
A LITTLE WHIPPED CREAM
GRATED NUTMEG

Whisk the eggs with the honey and salt. Pour on the scalded milk and vanilla, and beat until frothy. Add the rum if using, then pour into 2 mugs or glasses. Top with a dollop of whipped cream and sprinkle with grated nutmeg.

MAKES 2 MUGS

DESSERTS

Luscious soft fruits of summer, crisp apples and pears, juicy oranges, tangy lemons, tropical fruits—all make lovely ices, jellies, pies and tarts, or a tender mousse. Proper puddings that remind us of our youth, old favourites such as a golden steamed pudding or an apple charlotte, just never lose their appeal. The triumph of a perfect soufflé, the luxury of homemade ice cream, a lacy French crêpe or a creamy delicate bavarois can all crown a reputation as a fabulous cook.

Fresh Fruits Set in Wine Jelly

The combination of fruits used for a jelly such as this is entirely up to you—and the season. Summer berries are beautiful; so is the combination of pitted grapes and diced fresh mango. Mandarin or carefully peeled orange and pink grapefruit segments are good, too.

3 TABLESPOONS SUGAR
3 CUPS (24 FL OZ) FRUITY WHITE WINE
30 G (1 OZ) POWDERED GELATINE
2 CUPS (16 FL OZ) PREPARED FRUIT (A MIXTURE
    OF HULLED STRAWBERRIES, RASPBERRIES AND
    BLUEBERRIES (BILBERRIES) OR A COMBINATION
    OF FRUITS SUCH AS SEEDED GRAPES, DICED MANGO,
    APRICOT SLICES, ORANGE OR MANDARIN SEGMENTS).

Dissolve the sugar in 1 cup (8 fl oz) of the wine over a gentle heat. Add the gelatine and stir to dissolve thoroughly. Pour this mixture into the remaining wine in a bowl, stir gently with a spoon and place in the refrigerator until cold but not set.

Wet a 5-cup (2-pint) jelly mould or metal ring tin (tube pan or cake mould) and pour in about 5 mm (¼ in) of the wine mixture. Chill until set to a jelly. Scatter some of the fruits over this layer of jelly and carefully pour a little more wine mixture over. Return to the refrigerator until set. Continue making layers of fruit and jelly this way until all the wine jelly mixture is used and the mould is full. Leave in the refrigerator for several hours until set firm.

Dip the base of the mould into a bowl filled with very hot water for 2 seconds only, then carefully invert the jelly onto a wetted serving plate. (The base now becomes the top.) If the jelly does not slip out, give the mould a sharp shake; this will help release the jelly.

Decorate the top, if liked, with extra fruit and mint or strawberry leaves and serve.

SERVES 6–8

Overleaf: Fresh Fruits set in Wine Jelly can be made using a variety of fruits in different combinations.

Tamarillos with Crème Pralinée

8 TAMARILLOS (TREE TOMATOES)
1 CUP (8 OZ) SUGAR
2 CUPS (16 FL OZ) WATER
1 VANILLA BEAN
CRÈME PRALINÉE
4 EGG YOLKS
2 TABLESPOONS CASTER (SUPERFINE) SUGAR
1 TABLESPOON CORNFLOUR (CORNSTARCH)
600 ML (2½ CUPS, 1 IMP. PT) (LIGHT WHIPPING)
    CREAM, OR HALF CREAM AND HALF MILK
VANILLA ESSENCE (EXTRACT), TO TASTE
1 QUANTITY PRALINE (PAGE 168)

Drop half of the tamarillos in a saucepan of boiling water. Lift them out immediately with a slotted spoon and drop them into a bowl of cold water. Carefully slip off the skins. Leave the stalks intact, if possible. Repeat with the remaining tamarillos.

Place the sugar, water and vanilla bean in a medium saucepan. Heat gently until the sugar has dissolved. Bring to the boil and cook for about 2 minutes. Gently cook the tamarillos in this syrup until just tender, about 5 minutes. Remove from the heat and leave to cool.

Arrange the tamarillos in a serving dish, pour over some of the syrup and remove the vanilla bean. Serve with the Crème Pralinée.

Crème Pralinée. Place the egg yolks in a bowl with the caster sugar and cornflour. Whisk together until thick and pale. Scald the cream and pour it over the yolk mixture, stirring. Return this mixture to the saucepan, add vanilla essence to taste and stir over a very gentle heat until thickened enough to coat the back of the spoon. Remove from the heat and leave to cool, stirring frequently. Pour into a serving dish and leave to cool completely, then chill in the refrigerator.

An hour before serving, sprinkle a thick layer of the Praline powder over the top of the cream. The rest can be served separately.

SERVES 6–8

Lemon Parfaits

½ CUP (4 FL OZ) LEMON JUICE

1 TABLESPOON GRATED LEMON RIND

3 LARGE EGGS, SEPARATED

⅔ CUP (5 OZ) SUGAR

1 CUP (8 FL OZ) CHILLED (DOUBLE, WHIPPING) CREAM

LEMON RIND, SLIVERED, TO DECORATE

In a small, heavy, enamelled saucepan, combine the lemon juice and rind with the egg yolks and half the sugar. Beat the mixture well, then stir over a gentle heat until thickened without letting it boil. Set aside to cool.

Beat the egg whites until they hold soft peaks, then beat in the remaining sugar until the whites hold stiff peaks. Fold the whites into the lemon mixture.

Whip the cream until stiff and fold into the lemon meringue mixture. Turn the mixture into stemmed glasses and place in the refrigerator for a few hours until ready to serve.

SERVES 4–6

Iced Oranges

Very simple but very refreshing, especially after a fairly rich meal. It's a favourite finish to a meal in the Middle East.

1 CUP (8 FL OZ) ORANGE JUICE

3 TABLESPOONS FRESH LIME OR LEMON JUICE

3 TABLESPOONS HONEY

6 ORANGES

1 TABLESPOON ORANGE BLOSSOM WATER OR
    ROSE-WATER

GROUND CINNAMON, FOR SPRINKLING

Stir the fruit juices and honey together until the honey has dissolved. Peel the oranges, removing all the pith and keeping the oranges in their round shapes. Cut between the membrane to remove segments, or cut into rounds. Do this over the bowl of syrup to catch the juice. Remove any seeds.

Arrange the orange segments or slices in a pretty glass serving bowl and sprinkle with the orange blossom water or rose-water. Spoon the syrup over and sprinkle with the ground cinnamon. Chill before serving.

SERVES 6

Gratin of Fruits

A specialty of many top restaurants and a lovely dinner party dessert.

2–4 SWEET, JUICY GRAPEFRUIT

2–4 ORANGES

2 EGG YOLKS

1 TABLESPOON CASTER (SUPERFINE) SUGAR

1 CUP (8 FL OZ) CRISP, DRY CHAMPAGNE-STYLE
    WINE

ICING (CONFECTIONERS') SUGAR, FOR SPRINKLING

FRESH FRUIT AND MINT LEAVES, TO DECORATE

Peel the grapefruit and oranges, removing all the pith, and cut into segments away from the membrane. Arrange on four heatproof serving plates.

Whisk the egg yolks and sugar together in a bowl over a pan of simmering water. Whisk in the champagne and continue to beat until the mixture is light and fluffy, and slightly thickened. Remove from the heat and continue to whisk until cooled slightly.

Spoon the sauce over the fruit, sprinkle lightly with icing sugar, and place under a preheated, very hot grill (broiler) for a few moments until lightly coloured. Decorate with fresh fruit and mint leaves.

SERVES 4–6

The vanilla bean is unequalled for flavouring desserts, cakes and custards. When used to flavour custards and other sweet sauces, the bean is scalded with cream or milk, and left to infuse until the liquid cools. It can be used again if washed and dried. Vanilla beans are best stored in the freezer.

Summer Pudding

Most good greengrocers have fresh raspberries during the summer months. Look also for redcurrants. These two fruits are traditionally used in a summer pudding. If you have no luck with fresh berries, try the frozen ones from large food stores. Summer Pudding needs to be made at least a day before it is to be served.

½ LOAF UNSLICED WHITE BREAD, CUT INTO THICK
    SLICES, CRUSTS REMOVED
750 G (1½ LBS) MIXED FRUIT, CHOOSING FROM
    STRAWBERRIES, RASPBERRIES, BLUEBERRIES
    (BILBERRIES), OR OTHER BERRY FRUITS,
    REDCURRANTS, BLACKCURRANTS, STONED
    (PITTED)CHERRIES
⅔ CUP (5 OZ) SUGAR

Reserve two slices of bread; cut the rest into wedges or oblongs and use them to line the base and sides of a 4-cup (1¾-pint) charlotte mould or pudding basin.

Place the fruit and sugar in a heavy-based saucepan, cover and cook over a low heat for 5 minutes, stirring occasionally, very gently. This encourages the fruit juices to flow. Allow to cool.

Spoon the fruit into the pudding basin and lay the reserved slices of bread on top. Spoon any remaining fruit juice over, reserving 1–2 tablespoons for coating any patches once the pudding is turned out.

Place a small, flat plate on top of the pudding, making sure it sits inside the basin. Place weights or heavy cans (about 1 kg/2 lbs) on top to compress the pudding, and place the basin on a large plate to catch any juices. Refrigerate overnight.

Turn out onto a plate. Serve with a bowl of cream separately, if liked.

SERVES 8

Summer Pudding is the ultimate dessert in summertime, when raspberries and redcurrants are plentiful.

Peach and Plum Compote with Sauce Sabayon

Clingstone peaches and the little plums that never seem to ripen are perfect for a hot compote. The French flavour the syrup with a vanilla bean, the Italians prefer the rind of a lemon or orange. Take your pick.

1 CUP (8 OZ) SUGAR
1 CUP (8 FL OZ) WATER
1 VANILLA BEAN, OR THE PARED RIND OF 1 LEMON
    OR ORANGE
4 PEACHES
4 PLUMS
SAUCE SABAYON
2 EGG YOLKS
1 TABLESPOON CASTER (SUPERFINE) SUGAR
½ CUP (4 FL OZ) SWEET SHERRY

Dissolve the sugar in the water with the vanilla or rind over gentle heat and simmer for 5 minutes to make a syrup. To peel the peaches and plums first pour boiling water over them and leave them to stand for 3 minutes, then drain and remove the skin. Drop the fruit into the syrup and poach gently until the fruit is tender. Serve warm with the Sauce Sabayon.

Sauce Sabayon. Put the ingredients together in a bowl and stand the bowl in a saucepan of simmering water. Whisk briskly until the sauce becomes thick and mousse-like. Don't allow the water to boil or the sauce will curdle. Serve immediately, pouring over each serving of fruit.

SERVES 4–6

Gratin of Oranges and Capsicums

An unusual combination of glacé red and green capsicums (sweet peppers) and fresh orange segments makes a fabulous, fresh-tasting dessert for special occasions. The dessert is grilled (broiled) lightly with a Chantilly cream just before serving. For a simpler and even more refreshing version, serve the orange and capsicum cold without the cream and gratin finish.

1 RED CAPSICUM (SWEET PEPPER)
1 GREEN CAPSICUM (SWEET PEPPER)
3 CUPS (1½ LBS) SUGAR
1¼ CUPS (10 FL OZ) WATER
1½ TABLESPOONS LIQUID GLUCOSE
6–8 ORANGES
½ CUP (4 FL OZ) GRAND MARNIER OR COINTREAU
2½ CUPS (1 IMP. PT) (LIGHT WHIPPING) CREAM
½ CUP (4 OZ) CASTER (SUPERFINE) SUGAR,
    PREFERABLY SUGAR THAT HAS BEEN STORED WITH
    A VANILLA BEAN
¾ CUP (3 OZ) FLAKED (SLICED) ALMONDS, LIGHTLY
    TOASTED

Blanch the capsicums for 3 minutes in boiling water; drain and refresh under cold water. Cut into rings, removing the seeds and stalk.

Put the sugar, water and glucose in a saucepan and bring to the boil, stirring to ensure that all the sugar has dissolved. Boil until 'large ball' stage is reached, just between 'soft ball' and 'hard ball' on a sugar thermometer. If you don't have a sugar thermometer, test by dipping a wooden skewer into water, then into the syrup and then back into the water; if you can roll the resulting syrup into a soft ball, it is ready.

Add the capsicum rings and cook over a gentle heat until 'glacéed', about 35 minutes. Cool them in the syrup. They are better made well in advance.

Meanwhile, peel the oranges, removing all the pith, and cut into segments from between the membranes. Put the segments in a bowl with the Grand Marnier or Cointreau, and leave them to macerate while waiting to serve. Whip the cream with the caster sugar, but not too firmly.

To serve, arrange the orange segments on dessert plates with a border. Sprinkle with the almonds and arrange a little glacé capsicum in the centre of each. Spread with a thin layer of the sweetened whipped cream and place under a preheated grill (broiler) until lightly coloured.

SERVES 6–8

Autumn Fruit Compote

This compote is served barely warm, before the small amount of butter used has had a chance to solidify.

2 GOLDEN DELICIOUS APPLES
1 FIRM, RIPE PEAR
3 ORANGES
3 TABLESPOONS LEMON JUICE
2 TABLESPOONS UNSALTED BUTTER
3 TABLESPOONS ORANGE MARMALADE

Peel the apples and pear and cut into eighths. Toss them in the lemon juice. Peel the oranges, removing all the pith, and cut into segments between the membranes.

Heat a frying pan (skillet) with 1 tablespoon of the butter and sauté the apple and pear gently until tender. Transfer to a bowl. Add the marmalade to the pan with the remaining butter and cook, stirring all the time, until the marmalade has melted. Pour this over the sautéed fruit.

Gently toss the orange segments with the apple and pear and spoon into serving bowls.

SERVES 4–6

Apples for use in pies, puddings and compotes should not be put into cold water after slicing. While this may preserve their whiteness, it is at the expense of flavour.

Passionfruit Soufflé Crêpes with Tamarillo Sauce

½ CUP (4 FL OZ) PASSIONFRUIT PULP

4 TABLESPOONS ICING (CONFECTIONERS') SUGAR

2 EGG YOLKS

1 TABLESPOON ORANGE JUICE

6 EGG WHITES

EXTRA 2 TABLESPOONS ICING (CONFECTIONERS')
    SUGAR

12 OR MORE CRÊPES (PAGE 101), ABOUT 23 CM
    (9 IN) IN SIZE, WARM

TAMARILLO SAUCE

3 TAMARILLOS (TREE TOMATOES), SLICED THICKLY

¾ CUP (6 FL OZ) WATER

4 TABLESPOONS SUGAR

Preheat the oven to 220°C (425°F).

Put the passionfruit pulp, icing sugar, egg yolks and orange juice in a large bowl and mix until the ingredients are well combined. Beat the egg whites until soft peaks form, then beat in the extra 2 tablespoons of icing sugar until thick. Stir the egg whites left on the whisk into the passionfruit mixture and when combined fold the remaining whites in gently.

Butter a shallow ovenproof serving platter lightly. Spoon an equal amount of the egg and passionfruit mixture into the centre of each crêpe. Fold the part nearest you over the centre, turn in the sides and flip the further side over (this takes a little practice at first). Arrange the crêpes folded side down on the buttered platter and place in the oven for 4–5 minutes until nicely risen. Serve immediately with the Tamarillo Sauce.

Tamarillo Sauce. Put the tamarillos in a saucepan with the water and sugar, and cook gently until soft. Drain the fruit from the syrup, reserving the syrup, and rub through a sieve to make a purée. Pour the purée into a bowl and stir in enough reserved syrup to make the desired sauce consistency.

SERVES 6

Strawberry Galette Hearts

A light almond and hazelnut meringue sandwich filled with strawberries and cream. The galette hearts can be made a few days ahead and then freshened in a moderate oven before filling.

2 EGG WHITES

1 TABLESPOON PLAIN (ALL-PURPOSE) FLOUR

3 TABLESPOONS EACH GROUND HAZELNUTS AND
    GROUND ALMONDS

3 TABLESPOONS CASTER (SUPERFINE) SUGAR

30 G (1 OZ) BUTTER, SOFTENED

WHIPPED CREAM FLAVOURED WITH VANILLA ESSENCE
    (EXTRACT) AND ICING (CONFECTIONERS') SUGAR

SLICED STRAWBERRIES

ICING (CONFECTIONERS') SUGAR, SIFTED, FOR
    DUSTING

COULIS (PAGE 166), FOR SERVING (OPTIONAL)

Preheat the oven to 180°C (350°F). Use a large heart-shaped cutter or cardboard stencil to mark eight heart shapes on two pieces of baking paper (parchment).

Whisk the egg whites until stiff and dry. Sift the flour into the egg whites and add the ground nuts and sugar with the softened butter. Gently fold to combine.

Spread the mixture on the marked heart shapes placed on baking trays (sheets). Bake for about 20 minutes, until pale golden. Place on wire racks to cool. Trim the edges with cutters to re-form the heart shapes if necessary; they will have spread slightly. Remove the paper.

Place a heart on each dessert plate and cover with the whipped cream and strawberries. Top with another heart and dust with sifted icing sugar. If liked, place on top a strawberry that has been sliced not quite through and opened out into a pretty fan shape. Surround with a little coulis.

SERVES 4

Fresh Lemon Jellies

3 TABLESPOONS COLD WATER

1½ TABLESPOONS POWDERED GELATINE

2 CUPS (16 FL OZ) BOILING WATER

½–¾ CUP (4–6 OZ) SUGAR (TO TASTE)

A PINCH OF SALT

3 JUICY LEMONS

1 TEASPOON GRATED LEMON RIND

GERANIUM LEAVES OR BAY LEAVES, WELL WASHED,
   TO DECORATE

Pour the cold water into a small saucepan and sprinkle over the gelatine. Heat very gently and stir lightly until the gelatine has dissolved. Pour in the boiling water, sugar and salt and continue stirring until thoroughly mixed.

Halve the lemons lengthwise for squeezing and, once squeezed, scoop out and discard the insides. When the jelly liquid has cooled slightly, stir in the grated rind and the strained lemon juice. Pour into the lemon halves (or into a wet mould) and chill until the jelly is firm.

Cut each lemon half into two wedges (or dip the bottom of the mould into hot water for a couple of seconds and invert onto a plate). Serve on a platter lined with the geranium or bay leaves.

SERVES 4

Right: Fresh Lemon and Orange Jellies were a traditional feature of the English Christmas table.
Below: Gratin of Oranges and Capsicums (page 88) is an elegant dessert. It can be finished with cream and grilled or left uncooked.

Almond Jelly with Lychees

½ CUP (2 OZ) GROUND ALMONDS

2½ CUPS (1 IMP. PT) WARM WATER

150 ML (5 FL OZ) EVAPORATED MILK

3 TABLESPOONS CASTER (SUPERFINE) SUGAR

2 TABLESPOONS POWDERED GELATINE MIXED WITH
   4 TABLESPOONS WATER

A FEW DROPS OF ALMOND ESSENCE (EXTRACT)

½ CUP (4 OZ) SUGAR (OPTIONAL)

2 CUPS DRAINED CANNED OR FRESH PEELED LYCHEES

Infuse the ground almonds in the warm water, covered, for about 30 minutes, then strain through a sieve lined with muslin (cheesecloth). Mix the strained liquid with the evaporated milk and caster sugar in a saucepan and heat gently to dissolve the sugar. Cool slightly.

Dissolve the gelatine over a pan of hot water and, when clear, stir all at once into the almond-milk mixture. Cool and add almond essence to taste. Pour into a wetted shallow dish so that the jelly will be 2 cm (¾ in) thick and chill until set and firm.

If using fresh fruit, make a syrup by dissolving the sugar in 1 cup (8 fl oz) of water and boiling for a minute or so. Cool.

Cut the jelly into 2 cm (¾ in) wide diamonds and arrange in a bowl with the peeled or canned fruit. If using fresh fruit, add the prepared syrup; if using canned fruit, use the syrup from the can. Stir very gently to mix.

SERVES 6

Ice Cream

If you love the flavour of real ice cream made at home, a French 'sorbetiere' is a worthwhile investment. It does away with the buckets of ice and the rock salt by doing the job of churning in your freezer. It is an oblong aluminium tray with a fitted lid and a small motor and plastic paddles. The flat cord fits out of the closed freezer door to plug into a power point. Once it is frozen the motor automatically switches off.

It's also perfectly possible to make delicious creamy ice cream in the ice trays of your freezer, especially if you choose a recipe with a thick custard base. Whichever way you make them, the following recipes produce ice creams with a delicious rich, smooth creaminess.

Italian Coffee Ice Cream

No ice cream maker is necessary to make this ice cream smooth and creamy. The mixture itself ensures its rich, velvety texture.

6 EGG YOLKS
½ CUP (4 OZ) CASTER (SUPERFINE) SUGAR
2 CUPS (16 FL OZ) (LIGHT WHIPPING) CREAM
1½ CUPS (4 OZ) COFFEE BEANS, VERY LIGHTLY CRUSHED

Beat the yolks with the sugar until light and pale in colour. Scald the cream with the coffee beans and pour onto the yolk mixture, stirring until well combined. Pour the mixture back into the saucepan and stir over a gentle heat until the mixture thickens and coats the back of a spoon. Allow the mixture to cool, leaving the beans in the custard to infuse.

Strain into a chilled ice cream tray and cover with foil. Place in the freezer turned to its coldest setting and freeze.

Serve with fruit or a crisp dessert biscuit.

SERVES 6–8

Coconut Ice Cream

Serve this with spears of fresh pineapple to round off your next curry meal. Actually it's good at any time.

1½ CUPS (12 FL OZ) EACH (DOUBLE, WHIPPING) CREAM AND MILK
1 CUP (3 OZ) DESICCATED (SHREDDED) COCONUT
2 EGGS
2 EGG YOLKS
½ CUP (4 OZ) SUGAR
A PINCH OF SALT

In a medium saucepan, scald the cream and milk together with the coconut over a very gentle heat; this should take about 15 minutes. Cover and cool thoroughly. Blend in a food processor and rub through a sieve to extract as much of the coconut as possible. Discard the residue.

Using an electric whisk, beat the eggs and yolks together with the sugar and salt in a heatproof bowl until thick and mousse-like. Place the bowl over a saucepan of simmering water, then stir in the coconut milk. Cook, stirring often, until thick enough to coat the back of the spoon. Remove from the heat and place in a pan of ice-cold water, stirring occasionally until cooled.

Freeze in an ice cream maker according to manufacturer's instructions, or pour into a metal ice cream tray, cover with foil and place in the freezer turned to its coldest setting. When firm, store in the freezer at normal setting.

Scoop into bowls and decorate, if liked, with lightly toasted shredded coconut.

SERVES 4–6

Ginger Rum Ice Cream

While you're at it, try doubling this recipe, it's so good.

½ CUP (4 OZ) SUGAR
1 CUP (8 FL OZ) MILK
1 CUP (8 FL OZ) (LIGHT WHIPPING) CREAM
4 LARGE EGG YOLKS
3 TABLESPOONS DRAINED PRESERVED GINGER, CUT
    INTO SMALL PIECES
3 TABLESPOONS DARK RUM

Heat the sugar, milk and cream in a saucepan over a moderate heat, stirring until the milk and cream are scalded and the sugar has dissolved. In a bowl, beat the egg yolks until light and thick, and blend in the hot milk and cream mixture, stirring all the time. Return to the saucepan and stir over a gentle heat until the custard has thickened, without boiling. Leave to cool thoroughly.

Stir the ginger into the cooled custard with the rum. Freeze in an ice cream maker according to manufacturer's directions, or pour into an ice cream tray, cover with foil and place in the freezer turned to its coldest setting. When using a tray, check to see if the semi-frozen ice cream is too icy; if so, transfer it to a bowl and beat with an electric whisk until creamy, then return it to a tray, cover with foil and continue to freeze until firm.

SERVES 6

To prevent ice cream forming crystals, turn the freezer up to maximum 30 minutes before placing in the ice cream mixture. The temperature can be reduced to normal after 1–1½ hours.
Ideally, ice cream should be stored at a fairly low temperature, between -23°C and -18°C (-10°–0°F), to maintain its fine texture. It should also be well covered so that the fat doesn't pick up odours from the rest of the freezer and the moisture doesn't settle on the surface and form large crystals.

Apricot Macaroon Ice Cream

1 CUP (2 OZ) DRIED APRICOTS
1½ CUPS (12 FL OZ) (LIGHT WHIPPING) CREAM
3 LARGE EGG YOLKS, BEATEN
½ CUP (4 OZ) SUGAR
60 G (2 OZ) ALMOND MACAROONS OR AMARETTI
    BISCUITS, CRUSHED
ORANGE-FLAVOURED LIQUEUR

Cook the apricots in a little water until they are tender. Drain and push the fruit through a sieve to make a thick purée.

In the top of a double boiler, gradually stir the cream into the beaten egg yolks and cook over gently simmering water, stirring constantly until thickened. Remove from the heat, add the sugar immediately and stir in the apricot purée. Add more sugar if necessary to taste.

Freeze in an ice cream maker according to manufacturer's instructions, adding the crushed macaroons or biscuits at this point. Alternatively, pour the ice cream mixture into a freezer tray and cover securely with foil, freeze until the ice cream forms a solid rim about 3 cm (1¼ in) wide, then transfer to a chilled bowl and beat with an electric whisk or rotary beater until smooth without melting. Now add the crushed macaroons or amaretti and return the mixture to the tray and freeze again until firm and creamy.

Serve with a little orange-flavoured liqueur splashed over it.

SERVES 4–6

Eggs in the Snow (Oeufs à la Neige)

This French classic is one of the most delectable of desserts. Mounds of meringue are poached in milk, then the milk is used to make a rich custard. (Alternatively the 'snow eggs' can be poached in gently simmering water, which some find easier). The mounds of soft meringue are set to float on the custard—they are often called 'îles flottantes', or 'floating islands'. Spun toffee, glacé cherries and angelica leaves turn this dish into a splendid Christmas dessert. If the day is humid, the toffee will melt quickly; in any case, it should be done at the last moment. If the toffee is a worry, use toasted flaked almonds instead. The custard and 'eggs' can be made hours before they are needed.

This dish can also be extended by soaking macaroons or sponge finger biscuits in a little fruit juice, wine or sherry in the base of the serving dish. They should be well soaked. Sliced strawberries can be added too, before the custard is poured in.

> 2½ CUPS (1 IMP. PT) MILK
> A PIECE OF VANILLA BEAN OR VANILLA ESSENCE (EXTRACT)
> 1 TABLESPOON PLUS ½ CUP (4 OZ) SUGAR
> 5 EGGS, SEPARATED
> 1 CUP (7 OZ) CASTER (SUPERFINE) SUGAR
> *TOFFEE*
> ½ CUP (4 OZ) CASTER (SUPERFINE) SUGAR
> 3 TABLESPOONS WATER
> A PINCH OF CREAM OF TARTAR
>
> GLACÉ CHERRIES OR STRAWBERRIES AND
>   ANGELICA LEAVES OR CEDRO (GLACÉ CITRON),
>   TO DECORATE

Put the milk, vanilla bean and 1 tablespoon of sugar into a wide, shallow pan and bring to simmering point. Whisk the egg whites until peaks form, then gradually beat in the caster sugar, a tablespoon at a time, until stiff peaks form and hold their shape.

Poach large tablespoons of the meringue in the simmering milk, turning to cook evenly, for 3–5 minutes or until set. Lift them out carefully with a slotted spoon, drain and set aside on a plate. Reserve the milk.

To make the custard, beat the egg yolks and the remaining ½ cup sugar together until thick and pale. Gradually stir in 1¾ cups (14 fl oz) of the hot milk with the vanilla bean. Pour the mixture into a saucepan and cook over gentle heat, whisking constantly, until the custard thickens sufficiently to coat the back of a wooden spoon. Do not allow to boil.

Remove from the heat and leave to cool for at least 15 minutes, stirring occasionally. Now remove the vanilla bean and pour the custard into a serving dish. Top decoratively with the meringue eggs and leave to cool completely.

Toffee. Combine the toffee ingredients in a small, heavy saucepan and cook over a gentle heat until the sugar dissolves. Continue cooking until the syrup turns a caramel colour.

Remove the toffee from the heat and drizzle over the snow eggs, topping each with a glacé cherry half or strawberries and leaves cut from angelica or cedro, if liked. Leave the toffee to set a minute or so before serving.

You may like to make a little spun sugar to finish the dessert. This is not as difficult as it appears. It should be done at the very last moment.

Set the pan of toffee in a larger pan of hot water. Coat the backs of two wooden spoons with the toffee, hold them back to back, then gently pull them apart. As threads begin to run, keeping pulling apart to give them length. Put the spoons together again and repeat, letting the threads come together at the ends and hang down in the middle. When you have enough, cut the threads off the thick toffee at the spoons, using scissors, and loosely drape and wind the threads over the dessert, giving it extra height.

SERVES 6

Eggs in the Snow, or Oeufs à la Neige, makes a splendid festive dessert for a celebration.

Rhubarb Bread Pudding

500 G (1 LB) RHUBARB

⅔ CUP (5 OZ) SUGAR

GRATED RIND OF 1 ORANGE

250 G (8 OZ) STALE FRENCH OR ITALIAN BREAD CUT
    INTO 2.5 CM (1 IN) CUBES

3 LARGE EGGS

2 CUPS (16 FL OZ) MILK

1 CUP (8 FL OZ) CREAM

FRESHLY GRATED NUTMEG

1 TABLESPOON BROWN SUGAR

½ TEASPOON GROUND CINNAMON

30 G (1 OZ) BUTTER

Combine the rhubarb with the sugar and orange rind in a ceramic or glass bowl and leave to macerate for 1 hour. Combine with the bread cubes. Butter a shallow baking dish and add the rhubarb and bread mixture. Preheat the oven to 150°C (300°F).

In a bowl beat the eggs until well blended. Scald the milk and cream and slowly pour the hot liquid into the eggs, beating well. Add the grated nutmeg and pour the mixture over the rhubarb and bread. Sprinkle with the brown sugar and cinnamon, and dot with the butter cut into small pieces. Place in a baking dish half-filled with hot water and bake, covered with greaseproof (waxproof) or baking paper (parchment), for 30 minutes. Remove the cover and bake for a further 30 minutes or until the custard is set.

SERVES 6

Firnee

This beautiful Indian sweet dish is as common to the people of India as rice pudding is to us.

3⅓ CUPS (1⅓ IMP. PTS) MILK

4 TABLESPOONS RICE FLOUR

1 TABLESPOON GROUND ALMONDS

4 CARDAMOM PODS, LIGHTLY BRUISED

1 TEASPOON ROSE-WATER

3 TABLESPOONS SUGAR

A FEW DROPS OF RED FOOD COLOURING

½ TEASPOON FRESHLY GROUND CARDAMOM

4 TABLESPOONS SLIVERED ALMONDS

1 TABLESPOON SLIVERED PISTACHIO NUTS

In a small bowl mix ½ cup (4 fl oz) of the measured milk with the rice flour and ground almonds. Place the remaining milk in a heavy saucepan with the cardamom pods and heat to boiling point, then gradually stir in the rice flour paste. Cook over gentle heat, stirring all the time until thickened.

Simmer gently for a few minutes, then stir in the rose-water and sugar, stirring until the sugar has dissolved. Now add the red food colouring to make the Firnee a very pale pink. Pour into small serving bowls (this should make about six). Sprinkle with the freshly ground cardamom, slivered almonds and pistachio nuts. Cool and chill until ready to serve.

SERVES 6

Omelette Soufflé

An omelette soufflé makes a lovely dessert which can be put together at a moment's notice with everyday kitchen ingredients. A good-quality jam (jelly or conserve) such as morello, homemade strawberry or apricot does much for the quality of the omelette.

Just as the savoury omelette opens the door to many flavour combinations, so too does the sweet omelette soufflé. Sliced strawberries with a little sugar to sweeten and a little grated orange rind and a squeeze of juice are lovely folded into an omelette soufflé. Try also sliced apples gently sautéed first in a little butter with brown sugar and grated lemon rind and then gently cooked until tender. For a spectacular effect, the omelette can also be dusted with icing sugar and flamed with a little heated rum.

3 EGGS
1 TABLESPOON CASTER (SUPERFINE) SUGAR
2 TEASPOONS PLAIN (ALL-PURPOSE) FLOUR
1 TABLESPOON (LIGHT WHIPPING) CREAM
GRATED RIND OF ½ LEMON
A PINCH OF SALT
15 G (½ OZ) BUTTER
2–3 TABLESPOONS JAM (JELLY), WARMED SLIGHTLY
ICING (CONFECTIONERS') SUGAR, SIFTED, FOR
   DUSTING

Preheat the oven to 190°C (375°F). Separate the egg whites from the yolks into a clean copper or china bowl. In another bowl, lightly beat the yolks with the sugar, flour, cream and lemon rind.

Whisk the egg whites with the salt until stiff peaks form. Pour into the yolk mixture and fold quickly and gently with a large metal spoon.

Heat the butter in a large ovenproof frying pan (skillet) and pour in the egg mixture. Place in the oven for 10–15 minutes or until risen and golden. Slide onto a heated serving dish and spread with warm jam. Fold over and sprinkle with sifted icing sugar.

For a lovely caramel lattice finish, heat some metal skewers over a naked flame until one end is red hot. Holding them with an oven mitt, burn the lattice design on the icing

sugar. The resulting caramel gives an interesting flavour to the omelette.

SERVES 2

Hot Chocolate Soufflés

125 G (4 OZ) DARK (SEMI-SWEET) CHOCOLATE
2 TABLESPOONS RUM OR COFFEE
4 EGGS, SEPARATED
1 EGG YOLK
4 TABLESPOONS SUGAR
1 CUP (8 FL OZ) CREAM, WHIPPED, TO SERVE

Preheat the oven to 190°C (375°F). Have ready four ¾-cup (6 fl oz) or six ½-cup (4 fl oz) soufflé dishes which have been buttered and dusted inside with sugar.

In a bowl over a pan of hot water, melt the chocolate with the rum or coffee. Beat the 5 egg yolks with the sugar until pale and thick. Beat in the chocolate mixture. Whisk the egg whites until stiff without being dry, and fold them into the chocolate mixture with a large metal spoon.

Three-quarters fill the prepared dishes with the batter and place them on a baking tray (sheet). Bake for 15–18 minutes until risen and crusty.

Serve immediately in the dishes placed on heated plates. Pass around the whipped cream for each guest to use: they should make a hole in the centre of their soufflé and fill it with cream.

SERVES 4–6

Most recipes for soufflés call for one egg white more than the quantity of yolks used. The egg whites are whisked until they stand in stiff peaks and then a spoonful is beaten into the basic soufflé mixture. The mixture is then folded into the remaining egg whites.

Hot Passionfruit Soufflés

If you can beat egg whites to a snow, you can make these soufflés; they are really very simple.

½ CUP (4 FL OZ) PASSIONFRUIT PULP, FRESH OR
    CANNED
4 TABLESPOONS SUGAR
1 TABLESPOON KIRSCH, ORANGE-FLAVOURED
    LIQUEUR OR BRANDY
A SQUEEZE OF LEMON JUICE
2 EGG YOLKS
4 EGG WHITES
WHIPPED CREAM, FOR SERVING
ICING (CONFECTIONER'S) SUGAR, FOR DUSTING

Preheat the oven to 200°C (400°F). Have ready six small buttered ovenproof soufflé dishes, or one large dish.

Purée the passionfruit in a food processor or blender, or rub through a coarse sieve. Add the sugar, liqueur and lemon juice. Beat the egg yolks until creamy and stir in the passionfruit syrup. Set aside.

Whisk the egg whites just until stiff peaks hold without looking dry. Stir a spoonful into the passionfruit mixture, then fold in the rest quickly and lightly. Spoon the mixture into the prepared soufflé dishes, levelling the top of each with a metal spatula.

Place in the oven and immediately reduce the temperature to 190°C (375°F). Bake for about 10 minutes, until well risen. Have ready a sifter with icing sugar to dust each soufflé and six heated plates to set them on. Cut off the side of each, if liked, and spoon in a little whipped cream. Dust again with icing sugar. Serve immediately.

SERVES 6

Berry Fruits with Sugared Yoghurt Cream

Rich, easy and delicious. The success of this dish depends on the quality of the fruits—they should be just perfect—and the yoghurt. Look for the best quality yoghurt, Bulgarian style for preference.

2 CUPS (16 FL OZ) QUALITY NATURAL (PLAIN)
    YOGHURT
300 ML (10 FL OZ) CREAM, WHIPPED
DARK BROWN SUGAR
DEMERARA OR RAW SUGAR
1 PUNNET (250 G/8 OZ) EACH STRAWBERRIES AND
    RASPBERRIES

Start a few hours before serving. In a bowl, fold together the yoghurt and whipped cream and turn into a fairly shallow serving dish. Sprinkle thickly with sugar, first with the dark brown sugar, then with the demerara, and spread it out with the palm of your hand to completely cover the top of the yoghurt cream. Cover with plastic wrap (cling film) and leave in the refrigerator for several hours. The sugars should seep into the yoghurt cream mixture and form a crust.

Hull the strawberries and halve or slice them thickly. Divide among four to six serving plates with the raspberries. Set a large scoop of the sugared cream alongside and serve. You may like to offer a dessert biscuit such as Cigarettes Russes (page 46) with this.

SERVES 4–6

Berry Fruits with Sugared Yoghurt Cream is a simply made dessert combining yoghurt, cream and brown sugar with berry fruits in season.

Hot Lemon Soufflé

The clear, sharp, fresh tang of lemons is good with almost any form of cookery, especially in a sweet dish. Nothing, for instance, could be more irresistible than a hot lemon soufflé straight from the oven.

OIL AND CASTER (SUPERFINE) SUGAR, FOR
    PREPARATION
45 G (1½ OZ) BUTTER
2 TABLESPOONS PLAIN (ALL-PURPOSE) FLOUR
1 CUP (8 FL OZ) MILK
¼ TEASPOON SALT
½ CUP (4 OZ) SUGAR
GRATED RIND AND JUICE OF 2 LEMONS
4 EGG YOLKS
5 EGG WHITES
ICING (CONFECTIONERS') SUGAR, SIFTED, FOR
    DUSTING

Make a band of doubled baking paper (parchment) about 10 cm (4 in) wide to fit around a 5-cup (2-pint) soufflé dish. Tie it around the dish with string and brush lightly with oil. Sprinkle the inside with caster sugar, tapping it to remove any excess. Preheat the oven to 180°C (350°F).

Melt the butter in a saucepan and blend in the flour; stir in the milk. When smooth, stir in the salt and sugar. Return to the heat, stirring the mixture until it boils. Add the lemon rind and juice.

Remove from the heat. Stir in the egg yolks. Beat the egg whites until stiff and fold into the lemon mixture with a large metal spoon, lightly and quickly. Pour into the prepared dish and place in the oven for about 30 minutes or until well risen and golden. Dust with a little icing sugar and serve immediately.

SERVES 4–6

Hot Vanilla Soufflé

Make the soufflé in one large dish or six individual dishes (these won't need a paper collar). Everyone must be seated ready for the soufflé as it comes from the oven. Scrape the seeds from the vanilla bean to extract as much of the fabulous flavour as possible.

OIL AND CASTER (SUPERFINE) SUGAR, FOR
    PREPARATION
45 G (1½ OZ) BUTTER
2 TABLESPOONS PLAIN (ALL-PURPOSE) FLOUR
1 CUP (8 FL OZ) MILK
¼ TEASPOON SALT
½ CUP (4 OZ) SUGAR
1 VANILLA BEAN, SPLIT
4 EGG YOLKS, LIGHTLY BEATEN
5 EGG WHITES
ICING (CONFECTIONERS') SUGAR, SIFTED, FOR
    DUSTING

Preheat the oven to 180°C (350°F). Make a band of doubled baking paper (parchment) about 10 cm (4 in) wide to fit around a 5-cup (2-pint) soufflé dish. Tie it around the dish with string and brush lightly with oil. Sprinkle the inside with caster sugar, tapping to remove any excess.

Melt the butter in a saucepan, stir in the flour off the heat, then cook for 1 minute. Remove from the heat and gradually stir in the milk. When smooth, stir in the salt, sugar and vanilla bean. Return to the heat and gradually bring to the boil, stirring constantly.

When the sauce has thickened, allow it to cool. Remove the vanilla bean and stir in the egg yolks. Beat the the whites until very stiff and stir a spoonful into the sauce to soften the mixture. Fold in the remaining egg whites lightly and quickly with a large metal spoon.

Pour the batter immediately into the prepared soufflé dish and bake for 35 minutes or until well risen and golden. Dust with a little icing sugar and serve immediately.

SERVES 6

Crêpes

1¼ CUPS (5 OZ) PLAIN (ALL-PURPOSE) FLOUR

A PINCH OF SALT

3 EGGS, LIGHTLY BEATEN

1½ CUPS (12 FL OZ) MILK (OR HALF MILK AND WATER)

1 TABLESPOON BRANDY

1 TABLESPOON MELTED BUTTER

EXTRA BUTTER, TO GREASE THE PAN

Sift the flour with the salt into a mixing bowl.
Make a well in the centre and add the eggs
and milk. With a wooden spoon gradually
draw in the flour. Beat well and stir in the
brandy and melted butter. Cover and leave to
stand for 1 hour.

Heat a little butter in a heavy frying pan
(skillet) or crêpe pan. Pour off the excess,
reserving it for when the pan needs
regreasing. Use a soup ladle to pour enough
batter to thinly coat the surface of the pan.
Rotate the pan quickly and run the batter
smoothly and evenly over the pan.

Pour off any excess batter. Cook until small
bubbles appear, about 1 minute, then use a
metal spatula to flip the crêpe over. Cook for
1 minute on the other side.

Stack the cooked crêpes flat with a small
square of greaseproof (wax) paper in between
each (this is optional) on a hot dish until they
are all made.

MAKES AT LEAST 12 CRÊPES

*A crêpe pan should be seasoned before use.
Half-fill it with oil, heat it very gently and
keep it over low heat for at least 30 minutes.
Remove the pan from the heat and leave the oil
in the pan overnight. Next day, pour off the oil
and wipe the pan with a kitchen paper towel.
After each use, dry the pan over gentle heat,
then brush it with a little oil.*

Treacle Sponge Pudding

*This pudding is equal favourite with Bread and
Butter Pudding for the title of the most fancied dessert
by men. Both are winners.*

2 TABLESPOONS GOLDEN SYRUP (LIGHT TREACLE)

JUICE OF ½ LEMON

1 TABLESPOON FRESH BREADCRUMBS

125 G (4 OZ) BUTTER

GRATED RIND OF 1 LEMON

½ CUP (4 OZ) CASTER (SUPERFINE) SUGAR

2 LARGE EGGS

1¼ CUPS (5 OZ) SELF-RAISING (SELF-RISING) FLOUR

A PINCH OF SALT

MILK

Butter a pudding basin and mix together the
syrup, lemon juice and breadcrumbs in the
base. In another bowl, cream the butter with
the lemon rind and gradually beat in the
sugar until light and fluffy. Add the eggs, one
at a time, beating well between each addition.

Sift the flour into the creamed mixture
with the pinch of salt, and fold in lightly with
just enough milk to form a batter that will
drop from the spoon. Turn the batter into the
prepared pudding basin, top with a round of
greaseproof (wax) paper and cover with
aluminium foil to come over the edges.
Secure with string.

Place in a saucepan that has been quarter-
filled with water, cover with a lid and steam
for 1½ hours. Check the water every now and
then, adding more if necessary during cooking
to prevent drying out.

Turn out the pudding and serve with more
golden syrup, warmed. Add a little lemon
juice to sharpen the taste, if liked.

SERVES 6

Golden Fruit Honey Pudding

The ultimate in delicious, sticky, fruity puddings so much in favour today in top restaurants and the home.

1¼ CUPS (5 OZ) PLAIN (ALL-PURPOSE) FLOUR, SIFTED

1½ TEASPOONS BAKING POWDER

⅔ CUP (4 OZ) DRIED SWEET APRICOTS, QUARTERED

¾ CUP (4 OZ) RAISINS

1 CUP (8 FL OZ) MILK

1 EGG

BUTTER, TO GREASE THE MOULD

¾ CUP (9 OZ) HONEY

Using your hand or a food processor, work the flour, baking powder and butter into a mixture that resembles coarse breadcrumbs. In a bowl, mix this with the apricots and raisins and, lastly, the milk and egg.

Grease a 4–5-cup (1½–2 pt) pudding basin. Put one-third of the honey in the bottom, then half the pudding batter followed by half the remaining honey. Put the remaining batter on top of that, press down well to remove any air pockets, and cover with the last of the honey. Snap on the pudding lid or cover with a large circle of greased baking paper (parchment)—make a pleat in the centre to allow room for rising, and tie with string. Place in a saucepan with enough boiling water to come halfway up the sides of the basin, cover and steam steadily for at least 3 hours. Keep topping up the water from a boiling kettle to prevent drying out.

Turn the pudding out onto a serving dish and serve with hot Crème Anglaise (page 165), or double (heavy whipping) cream.

SERVES 6

Bread and Butter Pudding with Sultanas

Even an old-fashioned bread and butter pudding has plenty of scope for cooks and chefs to update with their own special touch. This is a very popular pudding among men.

10–12 WHITE BREAD SLICES, CRUSTS REMOVED

60 G (2 OZ) BUTTER, SOFTENED

1 CUP (6 OZ) SULTANAS (GOLDEN RAISINS)

½ CUP (3 OZ) CURRANTS (OPTIONAL)

6 EGGS, LIGHTLY BEATEN

½ CUP (4 OZ) SUGAR

½ CUP (4 FL OZ) WHISKY OR SHERRY

1½ TEASPOONS GROUND MACE OR ½ TEASPOON
   NUTMEG

5 CUPS (2¼ IMP. PTS) MILK

1 TEASPOON GROUND CINNAMON

ICING (CONFECTIONERS') SUGAR, FOR DUSTING
   (OPTIONAL)

Preheat the oven to 190°C (375°F).

Butter the bread, cut into triangles and arrange half in a large buttered ovenproof dish. Scatter with half the dried fruit. Layer the remaining bread and fruit on top.

Beat the eggs with the sugar and whisky or sherry and mace or nutmeg. Scald the milk and pour into the egg mixture, mixing well. Strain over the bread triangles and soak for about 10–15 minutes. Sprinkle with cinnamon.

Set the dish in a roasting pan of hot water and bake until risen and golden, and a knife inserted in the centre comes out clean—about 1 hour. Dust with icing sugar, if liked, and serve.

SERVES 6

Golden Fruit Honey Pudding is rich with dried apricots, sultanas (golden raisins) and honey.

Apple Charlotte

This one of the nicest things one can do with apples. Reinettes or golden delicious apples are ideal. It is most important to cook the apple purée until it has an almost jam-like consistency, so that the charlotte retains its stately shape. A charlotte mould is deepish with sloping sides, and a lug on each side for grasping.

1.5 KG (3 LBS) APPLES
A SMALL NUT OF BUTTER
A STRIP OF LEMON PEEL
LIGHT BROWN SUGAR OR APRICOT JAM (CONSERVE), TO TASTE
WHITE SANDWICH BREAD, CRUSTS REMOVED
90 G (3 OZ) BUTTER, MELTED

Without peeling, core the apples and slice thickly. Place in a heavy saucepan with the nut of butter and the lemon peel. Cover tightly and cook gently until very soft. Rub through a coarse sieve and return to the pan with some brown sugar or apricot jam to sweeten. Cook rapidly, stirring all the time, until the mixture drops heavily from the spoon and leaves the sides of the pan, about 15 minutes.

Meanwhile, preheat the oven to 190°C (375°F). Cut the bread into strips about 4 cm (1½ in) wide and the length of your charlotte mould. Cut two rounds to fit the top and bottom of the mould (or you can use overlapping strips). Dip the bread into the melted butter and arrange overlapping strips around the sides of the mould. Place one round (or overlapping strips) in the base. Check at this point that there are no gaps for the apple purée to seep through. Fill with the purée and top with the last round of butter-dipped bread.

Bake for 40 minutes or so until the bread is thoroughly golden. It is important to have the bread crisp and golden or the charlotte will tend to break in the unmoulding and serving.

Unmould onto a serving dish and serve with softly whipped cream or a sauce made by melting apricot jam with water and sherry.

SERVES 8

Gingered Pecan Pear Crumble

1 KG (2 LBS) PEARS
3 TABLESPOONS BROWN SUGAR
2 TABLESPOONS FINELY CHOPPED PRESERVED GINGER
30 G (1 OZ) UNSALTED BUTTER, CUT INTO SMALL PIECES
2 TABLESPOONS LEMON JUICE
1 TABLESPOON PLAIN (ALL-PURPOSE) FLOUR
¼ TEASPOON EACH GROUND GINGER AND CINNAMON
CRUMBLE TOPPING
¾ CUP (3 OZ) PLAIN (ALL-PURPOSE) FLOUR
90 G (3 OZ) BUTTER, CUT INTO SMALL PIECES
½ CUP (4 OZ) SUGAR
1 CUP (4 OZ) CHOPPED PECANS

Peel and slice the pears and toss in a bowl with the brown sugar, ginger, butter, lemon juice, flour and spices. Turn into a deep pie dish.

Crumble Topping. Rub the flour and butter together until the mixture resembles coarse breadcrumbs, then stir in the sugar and pecans. Sprinkle the crumble over the pears, spreading it evenly.

Bake in a preheated oven at 190°C (375°F) for 45 minutes or until the pears are tender and the top is golden and bubbling.

SERVES 6

When making a moulded dessert with a cream base, first brush the mould with a little oil. For a gelatine base with no cream, the mould is just rinsed out with water and left wet. If the dessert is difficult to turn out of the mould, fill a large bowl with very hot water and dip the mould into it for a few seconds. This will loosen the contents and make unmoulding easier.

Fig and Raspberry Clafouti

This is a wonderful dessert, especially useful for those fortunate enough to have their own fig tree. Raspberries provide a little tartness to contrast with the luscious sweet figs.

500 G (1 LB) FRESH FIGS (ABOUT 9), HALVED
    LENGTHWISE
½ CUP (4 OZ) RASPBERRIES
3 TABLESPOONS BLANCHED WHOLE ALMONDS
2 TABLESPOONS PLAIN (ALL-PURPOSE) FLOUR
¾ CUP (6 FL OZ) MILK
½ CUP (4 OZ) SUGAR
2 LARGE EGGS
1 TABLESPOON PORT
¼ TEASPOON SALT
45 G (1½ OZ) UNSALTED BUTTER, COLD AND CUT
    INTO SMALL PIECES

Preheat the oven to 200°C (400°F). Arrange the figs decoratively, cut side up, in a buttered 5-cup (2-pint) gratin dish and scatter the raspberries around them.

In a blender or food processor, grind the almonds with the flour, then add the milk, 4 tablespoons of the sugar, the eggs, the port and the salt, and blend the custard well. It will be necessary to stop the motor and scrape down the sides every now and then. Pour the custard slowly over the fruit, dot the fruit with the butter and sprinkle with the remaining 2 tablespoons of sugar.

Bake the clafouti in the middle of the oven for 30–40 minutes or until the top is golden and the custard is set. Transfer it to a rack and let it cool for 20 minutes. Serve warm, with whipped cream if desired.

SERVES 4–6

Date Pudding with Caramel Sauce

250 G (8 OZ) PITTED DATES
1 TEASPOON GRATED GREEN GINGER OR
    ½ TEASPOON DRIED
1¼ CUPS (10 FL OZ) WATER
1 TEASPOON BICARBONATE OF SODA (BAKING SODA)
125 G (4 OZ) UNSALTED BUTTER
¾ CUP (6 OZ) CASTER (SUPERFINE) SUGAR
½ TEASPOON VANILLA ESSENCE (EXTRACT)
3 LARGE EGGS
2 CUPS (8 OZ) SELF-RAISING (SELF-RISING) FLOUR
1 TEASPOON GROUND GINGER
SAUCE
125 G (4 OZ) UNSALTED BUTTER
1 CUP (6 OZ) LIGHT BROWN SUGAR
3 TABLESPOONS (LIGHT WHIPPING) CREAM

Preheat the oven to 180°C (350°F). Butter and line a charlotte mould or 23 cm (9 in) cake pan with baking paper (parchment).

Place the dates, ginger and water in a saucepan and bring slowly to the boil. Stir in the bicarbonate of soda and set aside.

Cream the butter and gradually beat in the sugar until light and fluffy. Beat in the vanilla essence. Add the eggs one at a time, beating well after each addition. Sift the flour with the ground ginger and fold into the cream mixture. Lastly fold in the date mixture.

Turn the batter into the prepared pan and bake for 50 minutes until risen, golden and cooked when tested in the centre with a fine skewer. If the pudding is browning too much before it is cooked, cover with a doubled sheet of brown paper and continue cooking. Invert onto a heated serving plate.

Sauce. Melt the butter with the brown sugar and cream in a heavy saucepan. Allow to boil for 5 minutes before serving with the turned-out pudding.

SERVES 6–8

SWEET AND SAVOURY

The tradition of mixing sweet and savoury flavours goes back to ancient times. The Saracens created the early sweet–sour sauces for cooking meats. Romans added dates to vegetable caponatas. In the Middle East the wonderful fruit and meat stews called 'tagines' have been prepared for many generations.

Today, fruit, sugar and honey still add a welcome contrast to meats, poultry, fish and vegetable dishes.

Salad of Roasted Tomatoes with Shallots

This dish relies on flavoursome red tomatoes and delicious little golden shallots, both roasted in olive oil. Roasting brings out the natural sugars in the food.

8 GOLDEN SHALLOTS, PEELED AND HALVED

ABOUT 8 TABLESPOONS OLIVE OIL

2 TEASPOONS CASTER (SUPERFINE) SUGAR

8 RIPE TOMATOES, PEELED AND HALVED

1 TABLESPOON BALSAMIC OR WINE VINEGAR

SEA SALT AND FRESHLY GROUND PEPPER

BASIL LEAVES, TO GARNISH

Arrange the shallots on a sheet of aluminium foil, drizzle with 2 tablespoons of olive oil and the caster sugar. Fold up the sides of the foil and seal the edges to make an airtight parcel. Roast in a preheated oven at 200°C (400°F) for 45 minutes. Meanwhile, drizzle olive oil over the tomatoes and roast them in the oven for 20 minutes. Remove the tomatoes and shallots and set them aside.

Put the vinegar in a small bowl with salt and freshly ground pepper, and gradually whisk in 4 tablespoons of olive oil until a thickened dressing is formed. Whisk in the juices from the tomatoes.

Arrange the roasted tomatoes on a salad platter and spoon around the dressing. Top each tomato half with a shallot half and garnish with the basil leaves snipped into shreds with scissors.

SERVES 4–6

Pan-roasted Capsicums with Capers and Vinegar

Once you've tasted sweet red capsicums (sweet peppers) that have been scorched and peeled, and discovered how the flavour is transformed, you may not consider any other way of eating them. Here is a wonderful method of preparing capsicums which is very quick. They are fried in a hot pan so that the skin is scorched and the natural sugars are developed. This dish is best served cold.

ABOUT 6 WHOLE CAPSICUMS (SWEET PEPPERS), OF
   VARIOUS COLOURS

½ CUP (4 FL OZ) OLIVE OIL

3 LARGE GARLIC CLOVES, FINELY CHOPPED

2 TABLESPOONS CAPERS

2 TABLESPOONS WINE OR BALSAMIC VINEGAR

SALT

Halve the capsicums, flick out the seeds and cut into thick strips. Heat the oil in a wide frying pan (skillet) and stir-fry the pepper strips over a high heat.

When the skins have begun to scorch at the edges, add the garlic and capers. Fry for 30 seconds, then add the vinegar and salt.

Let the vinegar sizzle for a minute, then turn out the contents of the pan onto a serving dish. Serve with crusty bread.

SERVES 4–6

When buying capsicums (sweet peppers), avoid any that are wrinkled or have soft spots. They should be smooth, firm and gleaming. Store them in the refrigerator and use them within a week of purchase.

Overleaf: French-roasted Chicken with Pears can be made with golden delicious apples and cider as a substitute for the pears and wine.

Sweet and Sour Kidney Beans on Pumpkin Croûtes

This is a 'dressy' vegetarian dish using delicious butternut pumpkin.

2 x 440 G (15 OZ) CANS RED KIDNEY BEANS
1 ONION
4 TABLESPOONS OLIVE OIL
2 GARLIC CLOVES, CRUSHED
1 GREEN CAPSICUM (SWEET PEPPER), SEEDED AND
   DICED
2 TABLESPOONS LIGHT SOY SAUCE
1–2 TABLESPOONS CORNFLOUR (CORNSTARCH)
1 CUP (8 FL OZ) STOCK OR WATER
1 TABLESPOON TOMATO PASTE
1 TABLESPOON LIGHT BROWN SUGAR
1 TABLESPOON VINEGAR
1 BUTTERNUT PUMPKIN, PEELED AND CUT INTO
   1 CM (½ IN) SLICES
FRESHLY CHOPPED PARSLEY

Drain the beans, saving the liquid. Slice the onion and sauté it in half the oil until soft, about 5 minutes. Add the garlic and capsicum; cook another 2 minutes. Add the beans and stir-fry for 4 minutes. Add the soy sauce, the cornflour mixed with a little of the stock or water, and the remaining liquid, including the bean liquid. Stir in the tomato paste, sugar and vinegar and cook gently, stirring until the sauce has thickened. Add more cornflour or liquid as necessary—there should be just enough sauce to moisten the beans, but they should not be 'gluggy'.

Meanwhile, sauté the pumpkin slices in the remaining oil until golden on both sides and tender. Place a slice on each plate and top with the kidney beans and sauce. Scatter with chopped parsley.

SERVES 6

Ragout of Peas, Lettuce and Ham

One of the many rewards of sharing a house with children is that there is usually someone willing and with plenty of time to shell peas. So when peas are in season, there's no need to look for frozen peas; good as they are, they can't take the place of the wonderful fresh ones with all their sweetness and flavour. Younger peas need only a short time in boiling water before being drained and tossed in butter. This recipe is a way of using up older peas.

1 LARGE CRISP LETTUCE
90 G (3 OZ) BUTTER
1 KG (2 LBS) PEAS, SHELLED
ABOUT 12 SPRING ONIONS (SCALLIONS), PEELED
A HANDFUL OF PEA PODS
SALT AND FRESHLY GROUND PEPPER
125 G (4 OZ) LEG HAM, CUT INTO STRIPS
3 BREAD SLICES, CRUSTS REMOVED
OIL FOR FRYING
1–2 TEASPOONS SUGAR

Wash the lettuce thoroughly, discard the outer leaves and cut the head of lettuce into thick wedges. Melt 75 g (2½ oz) of the butter in a heavy saucepan and add the lettuce quarters, peas, spring onions and pea pods. Season well with salt and pepper and add about 3 tablespoons of hot water.

Cover with a tight-fitting lid and cook over gentle heat for about 30 minutes, shaking the pan from time to time. After 15 minutes, add the ham strips and continue cooking.

Meanwhile, cut each slice of bread into four triangles. Fry these in shallow oil until light golden on each side; drain. Just before serving, remove the pea pods from the pan and add the sugar and remaining 15 g (½ oz) of butter.

Turn the ragout into a hot serving dish and arrange the fried bread triangles around. If you are planning to serve this as an accompanying vegetable, the fried bread is not necessary.

SERVES 4–6

Danish Cucumber Salad

Cool, translucent cucumbers, thinly sliced and prepared with vinegar, a handful of snipped dill and a dash of sugar—a simple and refreshing salad, and a great addition to a buffet, especially with fish such as poached salmon.

1 LONG CUCUMBER, PEELED AND THINLY SLICED
1 TEASPOON SALT
2 TABLESPOONS TARRAGON VINEGAR
2 TABLESPOONS HOT WATER
2 TEASPOONS SUGAR
3 TABLESPOONS SNIPPED FRESH DILL

Sprinkle the cucumber with the salt and allow to stand for 30 minutes, then drain and turn onto a serving dish. Combine the vinegar, hot water and sugar and stir until the sugar has dissolved. Pour this liquid over the cucumbers and stir in the dill. Chill before serving.

SERVES 4–6

Elio's Homemade Olives

One of the most intriguing ways of offering olives, hot and sweet. Especially good with dry sherry. Sun-dried olives are available at specialty delicatessens.

250 G (8 OZ) SUN-DRIED OLIVES
1 TEASPOON CHOPPED GARLIC
½ TEASPOON CRUSHED CHILLI (CHILI PEPPER)
1 TABLESPOON SUGAR

Heat a frying pan (skillet) till smoking stage. Add the olives and heat them through. Add the garlic, then remove from the heat and add the chilli and sugar. Toss and serve in small bowl.

Italian Sweet and Sour Onions

It is worth making a big batch of these onions, as they keep very well in the refrigerator. They are great for giving a lift to a quickly made meal and make a lovely addition to a tray of antipasto dishes.

½ CUP (4 FL OZ) LIGHT OLIVE OIL
1 KG (2 LBS) PICKLING ONIONS OR SMALL ONIONS
   (OR LARGER ONIONS, QUARTERED), PEELED
JUICE OF 1 LEMON
¾ CUP (6 FL OZ) DRY WHITE WINE
2 TABLESPOONS WINE VINEGAR
A FEW SPRIGS OF PARSLEY
2 LARGE GARLIC CLOVES, PEELED
1 CUP (5 OZ) SULTANAS (GOLDEN RAISINS) OR
   CURRANTS
2 TABLESPOONS SUGAR
1 TEASPOON WHOLE BLACK PEPPERCORNS

Heat the oil in a large frying pan (skillet). When smoking, add the onions. Sauté quickly until pale golden all over, then add the lemon juice, wine and vinegar. Let it bubble, then add the remaining ingredients.

Return to the boil, cover and cook over a moderate heat for 5 minutes or so until the onions are crisp-tender, about 10 minutes. Remove the lid and allow the liquid to reduce until a syrupy sauce has formed. Cool and serve at room temperature.

SERVES 6

Italian Sweet and Sour Onions, using sweet onions, sultanas (golden raisins) or currants and sugar with tart wine vinegar, make a lovely antipasto dish.

Ants Climbing Trees

Perhaps this chilli dish of pork and noodles gets its charming name from the tiny pieces of minced pork apparently climbing the noodles.

250 G (8 OZ) MINCED (GROUND) LEAN PORK

2 TABLESPOONS LIGHT SOY SAUCE

1 TABLESPOON SUGAR

1 TEASPOON CORNFLOUR (CORNSTARCH)

½ TEASPOON CHILLI SAUCE

3 TABLESPOONS VEGETABLE OIL

1 SMALL RED CHILLI (CHILI PEPPER), CHOPPED

2 GREEN SHALLOTS (SPRING ONIONS, SCALLIONS),
    CHOPPED

90 G (3 OZ) CELLOPHANE NOODLES (RICE
    VERMICELLI), SOAKED IN WATER FOR 30 MINUTES

½ CUP (4 FL OZ) CHICKEN STOCK

SHREDDED GREEN SHALLOTS (SPRING ONIONS,
    SCALLIONS), TO GARNISH

In a small bowl, combine the minced pork with the soy sauce, sugar, cornflour and chilli sauce. Mix well and leave to marinate for about 20 minutes.

Heat the oil in a wok or large frying pan (skillet), add the chilli and chopped green shallots and stir-fry for a few seconds. Add the pork and continue to stir-fry until the pork changes colour. Drain the noodles, then add them to the pan. Stir-fry to blend; add the stock. Continue cooking until all the liquid is absorbed. Turn onto a serving plate and garnish with the shredded green shallots.

SERVES 4

Fried Spicy Green Beans

Much of South-East Asian cooking is a fine balance of sweet and sour–hot and spicy, also. It is this that makes the cuisine particularly attractive to the Western palate.

1 TABLESPOON VEGETABLE OIL

½ TEASPOON CUMIN SEEDS

4 GREEN CHILLIES (CHILI PEPPERS), SEEDED AND
    FINELY CHOPPED

500 G (1 LB) GREEN BEANS, ENDS AND STRINGS
    REMOVED, CUT INTO LONG DIAGONAL SLICES

1 TEASPOON SALT

2 TEASPOONS SUGAR

2 TABLESPOONS GRATED FRESH COCONUT (OR 1
    TABLESPOON DESICCATED (SHREDDED), LIGHTLY
    TOASTED)

¼ BUNCH FRESH CORIANDER (CHINESE PARSLEY),
    FINELY CHOPPED

Heat the oil in a wok or saucepan over a moderate heat. Add the cumin and chillies, and stir-fry for a few moments. Add the beans and stir-fry until bright green. Add the salt and about 4–5 tablespoons of water. Cover and cook until the beans are just tender. Add the sugar, mixing well.

Turn out onto a serving dish and sprinkle with coconut and chopped coriander.

SERVES 4

When seeding chillies (chili peppers), work under cold, running water. Make a slit down the side of the chilli and scrape out the seeds with the point of a knife. Take care not to touch your nose or eyes, as the juice will burn them. Always wash your hands well after handling chillies.

Before chopping or grinding chillies, tear each one into three or four pieces and soak them in hot water for 10 minutes. Squeeze out excess juices before using.

Pasta and Chicken Salad with Curry Dressing

Italy meets India in this unusual dressing, a combination that works very well.

250 G (8 OZ) SPIRAL-SHAPED PASTA SUCH AS
   ROTELLE OR FUSILLI
1 WHOLE CHICKEN BREAST, BONED, SKINNED AND
   POACHED
6 CHERRY TOMATOES, HALVED
3 GREEN SHALLOTS (SPRING ONIONS, SCALLIONS),
   FINELY SLICED
1 TABLESPOON SHREDDED BASIL LEAVES
DRESSING
1 SMALL GARLIC CLOVE
1 TEASPOON GRATED GINGER
1 TEASPOON CURRY PASTE
A PINCH OF CAYENNE PEPPER
1 TABLESPOON BUTTER
3–4 TABLESPOONS (LIGHT WHIPPING) CREAM
1 TABLESPOON WHITE VINEGAR
2 TABLESPOONS SWEET FRUIT CHUTNEY (MANGO OR
   PEACH IS GOOD)

Drop the pasta into boiling water and cook for 8–10 minutes until tender; drain. Refresh in a colander under cold water and drain thoroughly. Meanwhile, cut the poached chicken into chunks and put them in a bowl with the pasta, tomatoes, shallots and basil.

Dressing. Cook the garlic, ginger, curry paste and cayenne in the butter in a small pan until softened. Add the cream and cook, whisking until thickened slightly. Whisk in the vinegar and chutney.

Add the dressing to the pasta mixture with plenty of salt and freshly ground pepper, tossing the salad to combine well.

SERVES 4

Risotto with Tomatoes and Basil

Risotto cooked properly, the Italian way, is simply delicious. Risotto is a rich and creamy rice dish and should be made with a short-grain rice, preferably Arborio from Italy.

4–5 CUPS (1½–2 IMP. PTS) CHICKEN STOCK
60 G (2 OZ) BUTTER
1 TABLESPOON OIL
1 ONION, CHOPPED
750 G (1½ LBS) FIRM RIPE TOMATOES, SKINNED,
   SEEDED AND CUT INTO CUBES
SALT AND FRESHLY GROUND PEPPER
315 G (10 OZ) ARBORIO OR SHORT-GRAIN RICE
4 TABLESPOONS FRESHLY GRATED PARMESAN
   CHEESE
10 FRESH BASIL LEAVES, SHREDDED

Bring the stock to a simmer in a large saucepan. In another large, heavy-based pan, melt half the butter with the oil and gently sauté the onion until pale golden. Add the tomatoes, salt and pepper. Cook, stirring every now and then, for 5 minutes. Add the rice and stir a few times to coat thoroughly.

Add a ladleful of stock and stir constantly to keep the rice from sticking to the pan. Continue this process, adding a ladleful of stock at a time and stirring until the pan is dry again and the rice is tender. Add the remaining butter, cheese and basil. Stir and taste for salt and pepper. Serve as soon as possible.

SERVES 4

To peel tomatoes, cover them first with boiling water for 10 seconds, then place them under cold running water. Make a tiny slit in the skin at the base and strip the skin off towards the stem.

Roasted Capsicum and Tomato Tians

Look for yellow and red capsicums (sweet peppers); failing the yellow, select firm green ones. This dish, which is best served cold, needs plenty of crusty bread to mop up the delicious juices. I use individual soufflé dishes to prepare these.

3 LARGE RED CAPSICUMS (SWEET PEPPERS)

2 LARGE YELLOW CAPSICUMS (SWEET PEPPERS)

2 LARGE GARLIC CLOVES, CRUSHED WITH A LITTLE SALT

3 TABLESPOONS FRESHLY GRATED PARMESAN CHEESE

2–4 TABLESPOONS FRESH BREADCRUMBS

1 CUP (A GOOD HANDFUL) BASIL LEAVES, SHREDDED

2 SWEET SALAD ONIONS, FINELY SLICED

4–6 RIPE TOMATOES, SLICED

SALT AND FRESHLY GROUND PEPPER

1–2 TABLESPOONS OLIVE OIL

Char the capsicums over a gas flame or under a very hot grill (broiler), turning them all the time. Place in a paper bag and leave to cool. Scrape away the charred skin and rinse lightly in cold water. Halve them, remove the seeds and membranes, and cut the flesh into 2 cm (1 in) strips. Toss the strips with the crushed garlic. Combine the parmesan cheese and breadcrumbs with a little of the shredded basil.

Have ready six large ramekins or individual soufflé dishes and sprinkle a little breadcrumb mixture in each, using half in all. Layer two strips of red capsicum and one of yellow in the bottom to come up the sides of each dish and continue to layer the sliced onion, tomato, remaining capsicum strips and shredded basil until filled. Season with salt and pepper, top with remaining half of breadcrumb mixture and drizzle with oil.

Bake in a preheated oven at 190°C (375°F) for about 20 minutes. Remove from the oven and cool before chilling for several hours and serving.

SERVES 6

Caponata

This mixed vegetable dish from Sicily, which uses all the vegetables that grow so well around the Mediterranean, has a fabulous sweet and sour flavour. The addition of dates stems from Ancient Roman times. There are variations; sometimes green tomatoes are used instead of ripe ones.

2 EGGPLANTS (AUBERGINES), DICED

⅔ CUP (6 FL OZ) OLIVE OIL

2 RED CAPSICUMS (SWEET PEPPERS), SEEDED AND CUT INTO SQUARES

2 ONIONS, THINLY SLICED

4 TOMATOES, PEELED, SEEDED AND CHOPPED, OR 6 CANNED ITALIAN TOMATOES, DRAINED AND CHOPPED

2 TABLESPOONS DRAINED CAPERS

6–8 FRESH DATES, HALVED (OPTIONAL)

10 BLACK OLIVES, HALVED AND STONED (PITTED)

2 TABLESPOONS SUGAR

4 TABLESPOONS WINE VINEGAR OR 1 TABLESPOON BALSAMIC VINEGAR AND 3 OF WINE VINEGAR

SALT AND FRESHLY GROUND PEPPER

Sprinkle the diced eggplant with salt and leave to drain for 30–60 minutes. Heat half the oil in a deep frying pan (skillet). Sauté the cubes a few at a time until browned and soft, adding more oil as necessary. Remove the eggplant and repeat the process with the capsicums.

Put the eggplant back in the pan. Add the onions and tomatoes. Simmer for 15–20 minutes and then add the capers, dates (if using) and olives. Dissolve the sugar in the vinegar and add it to the pan. Season with salt and pepper, and simmer very gently for a further 20 minutes. Taste and add a little more vinegar if necessary. Cool and leave for several hours for the flavours to blend and mellow.

For a first course, serve cold with Italian bread. For a lunch or supper dish, serve with hard-boiled eggs, fried fish or grilled chicken.

SERVES 4

Caponata is a wonderful sweet and sour blend of Mediterranean vegetables flavoured with capers, dates, olives and vinegar.

Sugar-browned Potatoes

Caramelise potatoes as they do in Denmark, where they are a great favourite with ham and pork.

24 SMALL NEW POTATOES
½ CUP (4 OZ) CASTER (SUPERFINE) SUGAR
125 G (4 OZ) CLARIFIED BUTTER, MELTED

Boil the potatoes in their jackets for 10–15 minutes or until just cooked. Let them cool a little, then peel if the skins are not a good colour.

Melt the sugar in a heavy frying pan (skillet) over gentle heat. Continue to cook the sugar slowly until it becomes a light brown caramel, stirring to prevent it from burning. Stir in the butter and add as many potatoes as possible without crowding the pan. Shake the pan from time to time until the potatoes are coated with the caramel. Remove from the heat and serve as soon as possible.

SERVES 6–8

Moroccan-style Lamb Stew with Prunes

Sweet and spiced meats are something you expect in Morocco. Prunes give a rich quality to this lovely lamb dish. Serve it with steamed rice.

2 LARGE ONIONS, CHOPPED
2 LARGE GARLIC CLOVES, CRUSHED
3 TABLESPOONS OLIVE OIL
1½ KG (3 LBS) BONELESS LAMB SHOULDER, TRIMMED
    AND CUT INTO LARGE CUBES, AND THE BONE IF
    POSSIBLE
1 CINNAMON STICK
2 X 420 G (15 OZ) CANS TOMATOES, CHOPPED;
    JUICE RESERVED
SALT AND BLACK PEPPER
¼ TEASPOON SAFFRON THREADS
2 WHITE TURNIPS
6 PITTED PRUNES, HALVED

In a large, heavy saucepan, cook the onions and the garlic in the oil over a moderately low heat, stirring, until the onions are softened. Add the lamb and cook it over moderate heat, stirring, just until it is no longer pink. Stir in the cinnamon stick, the tomatoes with the reserved juice, 2 cups (16 fl oz) water, the lamb bone (if using) and salt and pepper to taste. Simmer the stew for 1 hour.

Stir the saffron into the stew. Peel the turnips, halve them horizontally, and cut each half into four wedges. Add the wedges to the stew and simmer for 30 minutes. Add the prunes and simmer the stew, covered partially, for 30 minutes, or until the lamb and the turnips are tender. Discard the lamb bone.

Serve the stew with steamed rice.

SERVES 6–8

Duck, Peach and Fresh Green Salad

Duckling is often served with fruit, which helps counteract the richness and extreme fattiness of the bird. Fresh cherries, orange or pineapple also may be used here.

2 KG (4 LBS) FRESH DUCKLING

A FEW CELERY LEAVES

A STRIP OF LEMON PEEL

SALT AND FRESHLY GROUND PEPPER

1 CUP (8 FL OZ) WHITE WINE

A SELECTION OF SALAD GREENS SUCH AS COS
    (ROMAINE), MIGNONETTE AND BUTTERHEAD
    LETTUCE, CURLY ENDIVE, CHICORY AND
    WATERCRESS

4–6 FRESH PEACHES, DEPENDING ON SIZE, CUT INTO
    WEDGES

DRESSING

2 TABLESPOONS EACH WHITE WINE VINEGAR AND
    ORANGE JUICE

A PINCH OF SALT

1 TEASPOON FRENCH OR DIJON MUSTARD

3 TABLESPOONS OLIVE OIL

Remove the neck from the duckling and place the celery leaves and lemon peel in the cavity. Season the outside with salt and pepper. Truss the duckling with string into a neat shape and place it on a rack in a baking dish.

Bake in a preheated oven at 200°C (400°F) for about 15 minutes. Pour off the fat and add the white wine to the baking dish. Cover the breast of the duck with a piece of foil or brown paper, and return the bird to the oven reduced to 180°C (350°F) for a further 1–1½ hours until tender. Remove from the oven to cool, then remove the string.

Carve the duck breast into long, thin slices and cut the leg and wing joints from the carcass. Line a serving platter with the salad greens and arrange the duck meat on top. Scatter the peach wedges over the duck.

Dressing. Mix the vinegar and orange juice with the salt and mustard, gradually whisking in the oil.

Spoon the dressing over the duck salad and serve at room temperature, not chilled.

SERVES 4

Sweet Potatoes and Apples

1 KG (2 LBS) SWEET POTATOES

2 RED APPLES, PREFERABLY JONATHANS

LEMON JUICE

60 G (2 OZ) BUTTER

½ TEASPOON SALT

½ CUP (3 OZ) (LIGHT) BROWN SUGAR

½ CUP (4 FL OZ) WATER

Peel the sweet potatoes and cut them into even-sized pieces. Place them in a saucepan of boiling water and simmer, covered, for 30 minutes or until tender. Drain and cool.

Wash and core the apples and cut them into thin slices. Sprinkle them with lemon juice to prevent them from discolouring.

Heat the butter, salt, sugar and water in a shallow pan and stir until the sugar dissolves. Boil for 3 minutes and then add the cooked sweet potatoes. Simmer for 3 minutes, basting frequently with the syrup. Add the apple slices and cook for a further 2 minutes.

SERVES 6

Sugar-roasted Prawns

12 LARGE RAW KING PRAWNS (JUMBO SHRIMP)
PEANUT OIL
4 THIN FRESH GINGER SLICES, FINELY CHOPPED
4 GREEN SHALLOTS (SPRING ONIONS, SCALLIONS),
   WITH GREEN TOPS FINELY CHOPPED
1 RED CHILLI (CHILI PEPPER), SEEDED AND CHOPPED
½ CUP (4 FL OZ) CHICKEN STOCK
½ TEASPOON SALT
¼ CUP (2 OZ) SUGAR
2 TEASPOONS SESAME OIL
CORIANDER (CHINESE PARSLEY) SPRIGS, TO GARNISH

Remove legs and feelers from the prawns,
leaving heads and shells intact. Heat 5 cm
(2 in) of oil in a wok or large, heavy frying
pan (skillet). Fry the prawns in the oil for
3–4 minutes or until they have turned pink.
Drain the prawns and set them aside.

Pour off the oil from the pan, leaving a thin
film. Stir-fry the ginger, shallots and chilli until
the mixture is fragrant, about 30 seconds, then
pour in the stock, adding the salt and sugar.
Cook over a very high heat so that the liquid
reduces rapidly. When the mixture starts to
caramelise, turn the heat to low and return the
prawns to the pan, stirring and turning them
over in the caramel so that they are well coated.
Sprinkle with sesame oil, and stir through.

Serve at once, garnished with coriander
sprigs. Serve with steamed rice, if liked.

SERVES 4

*Left: Sugar-roasted Prawns is a Chinese way of cooking
large king prawns (jumbo shrimp), often eaten using fingers.*

Buried Salmon (Gravlax)

Make this two or three days before you want to serve it.

750 G (1½ LB) PIECE OF SALMON OR OCEAN TROUT,
   USING TAIL PIECE OR MIDDLE CUT
3 TABLESPOONS FRESH CHOPPED DILL
1 TABLESPOON SEA SALT
1 TEASPOON COARSELY GROUND BLACK PEPPER
1 TABLESPOON SUGAR
1 TABLESPOON BRANDY

Cut the piece of fish into two fillets, removing
the backbone and any remaining little bones,
but leaving the skin intact. Put the first piece,
skin side up, in a dish into which the fillet just
fits. Mix the remaining ingredients together
and rub a third of the resulting pickle mixture
into the skin. Turn over, skin side down, and
rub another third of the pickle on top. On this
lay the remaining fillet, flesh side down. Rub
the last third of pickle into the skin of the top
piece. Cover tightly with aluminium foil and
press with a light weight.

Leave for 2–5 days in the refrigerator and
serve in thin slices as you would smoked
salmon. Accompany with rye, black or other
good bread, and with a mustardy mayonnaise
or one with grated horseradish added to taste.

SERVES 6–8

*Below: Gravlax from Sweden is marinated in sugar, salt
and brandy and eaten in thin slices with rye bread.*

Glazed Spatchcocks

I have made this dish as an alternative to turkey or duck for Christmas dinner. It is certainly festive enough for any special occasion

6 SPATCHCOCKS, EACH WEIGHING ABOUT 500 G (1 LB)
PARSLEY OR WATERCRESS TO GARNISH
STUFFING
3 GOLDEN SHALLOTS, FINELY CHOPPED
30 G (1 OZ) UNSALTED BUTTER
3 CUPS (6 OZ) LOOSELY PACKED DAY-OLD BREAD
 CUBES
1 CELERY STALK, FINELY CHOPPED
3 TABLESPOONS CHOPPED PINE NUTS
4 TABLESPOONS SULTANAS (GOLDEN RAISINS)
1 TEASPOON EACH GRATED ORANGE AND LEMON
 RIND
2 TEASPOONS FINELY CHOPPED SAGE
SALT AND FRESHLY GROUND PEPPER
½ CUP (4 FL OZ) DRY WHITE WINE OR ORANGE JUICE
60 G (2 OZ) UNSALTED BUTTER
GLAZE
3 TABLESPOONS SUGAR
1 TABLESPOON WHITE WINE VINEGAR
½ CUP (4 FL OZ) FRESH ORANGE JUICE
RIND OF ½ ORANGE, CUT INTO THIN MATCHSTICK
 STRIPS
3 TABLESPOONS MILD MANGO CHUTNEY

Rinse the spatchcocks and pat dry.

Stuffing. In a frying pan (skillet) cook the shallots in the butter over gentle heat until soft, about 5 minutes. Remove from the heat and add the remaining stuffing ingredients, mixing well.

Divide the stuffing among the cavities of the spatchcocks, packing it loosely. Truss each spatchcock into a neat shape with string. Season with salt and pepper and arrange on a rack in a large baking dish. Brush with the butter, melted and roast in a pre-heated oven at 200°C (400°F) for 30 minutes. Reduce heat to moderate 180°C (350°F) and roast for a further 15 minutes.

Glaze. In a small enamel or stainless steel saucepan dissolve the sugar and vinegar together and cook until a pale amber. Remove the pan from the heat, stir in the orange juice and rind and cook the mixture over a moderate heat until smooth. Stir in the mango chutney.

Brush the birds with the glaze and continue to roast for a further 30 minutes, basting again every 10 minutes or so.

To serve, remove the strings and arrange on a heated platter, garnishing with sprigs of parsley or watercress.

Breast of Chicken with Raspberry Vinegar

This lovely little dish uses wonderful homemade raspberry vinegar. A lovely sweet–sour combination.

4 CHICKEN BREAST HALVES, SKINNED
SALT AND FRESHLY GROUND PEPPER
60 G (2 OZ) BUTTER
1 SMALL RED ONION, FINELY CHOPPED
2 TABLESPOONS RASPBERRY VINEGAR (PAGE 154)
4 SPRIGS OF TARRAGON, TO GARNISH

Season the chicken lightly with salt and pepper. Melt half the butter in a heavy frying pan (skillet), add the chicken and brown lightly on all sides for 3–5 minutes. Cover and cook gently over low heat, for 5–8 minutes or until the chicken is cooked, but is still tender. Transfer to a serving dish, cover and keep hot while you make the sauce.

Add the onion to the juices in the pan and cook, stirring occasionally, for 5–6 minutes or until soft. Pour in the vinegar and cook over a high heat until the liquid is reduced and the sauce is slightly syrupy. Remove from the heat and add the remaining butter.

Slice the chicken on the bias and put on individual plates. Spoon the sauce to one side of the chicken. Garnish with the tarragon or other greens, such as watercress or arugula, and serve.

SERVES 4

Grilled Chicken Salad

Warm salads are just lovely, the freshly cooked food nestling on crisp salad greens and dressed with the warm pan juices and sweet–sour dressing.

4 CHICKEN BREAST HALVES
FRESHLY GROUND PEPPER
VIRGIN OLIVE OIL
DRESSING
¼ TEASPOON FRENCH MUSTARD
1 TABLESPOON BALSAMIC VINEGAR
2 TABLESPOONS WINE VINEGAR
1 TABLESPOON HONEY
½ CUP (4 FL OZ) VIRGIN OLIVE OIL
SALT AND FRESHLY GROUND PEPPER

A SELECTION OF SALAD GREENS SUCH AS WATERCRESS,
    ARUGULA, RADICCHIO, BUTTERHEAD LETTUCE OR
    MIGNONETTE, WASHED, DRIED AND TORN INTO
    SERVING-SIZE PIECES
¼ CUP (1 OZ) TOASTED WALNUTS OR PECANS
½ CUP (3 OZ) SULTANAS (GOLDEN RAISINS), SOAKED
    IN WATER TO JUST COVER

Remove any excess fat from the chicken breasts, leaving the skin and bone intact. Season with pepper and brush with the olive oil. Have ready a preheated grill (broiler) or ribbed grill pan and cook the chicken until tender, about 4–5 minutes on each side. Remove from the heat. As soon as it has cooled enough to handle, cut the flesh in one piece from the bone and then cut it into medium thick slices.

Dressing. Whisk together the mustard, vinegars and honey in a bowl and slowly add the olive oil, whisking all the time. Season with salt and pepper.

Toss the salad greens in the dressing and arrange on four serving plates. Place a sliced half-breast beside or on the greens, top with the toasted walnuts and drained sultanas, and drizzle with the hot chicken pan juices.

SERVES 4

Devilled Grilled Chicken

This recipe uses a fabulous devil mixture. The chicken is rubbed and marinated with dry spices and sugar, then finished off with a buttery and fruity sauce combination which is quite wonderful. Serve with a buttered rice pilaf.

6 LARGE CHICKEN PIECES, SUCH AS MARYLANDS
    (THIGH WITH DRUMSTICK) OR BREAST HALVES
2 TEASPOONS EACH SALT AND SUGAR
1 TEASPOON EACH GROUND PEPPER, GROUND
    GINGER AND DRY MUSTARD
½ TEASPOON CURRY POWDER
60 G (2 OZ) BUTTER
2 TABLESPOONS TOMATO CHUTNEY OR KETCHUP
1 TABLESPOON WORCESTERSHIRE SAUCE
1 TABLESPOON LIGHT SOY SAUCE
1 TABLESPOON FRUIT SAUCE OR CHUTNEY
A DASH OF TABASCO
SPRIGS OF CORIANDER (CHINESE PARSLEY) OR
    WATERCRESS, TO GARNISH

Wipe the chicken pieces and remove any excess fat. Mix the salt, sugar and spices together, and rub well into the entire surface of the chicken pieces. Leave to marinate for at least 1 hour.

Arrange the chicken pieces on the foil-lined rack of a grilling (broiling) pan and brush with the butter, which has been melted in a small pan. Cook the chicken under a preheated grill (broiler) for 10 minutes, turning once after 5 minutes. Keep a careful eye on the chicken to watch for burning, and cover with foil where necessary until the chicken is cooked.

Meanwhile, add the remaining ingredients to the butter in the pan and spoon the mixture over the chicken, turned skin side up. Continue to cook, basting with the mixture for a further 10 minutes or until the juices run clear when a thigh is pricked with a skewer.

Arrange on a platter, garnish with coriander or watercress, and serve.

SERVES 4–6

Roast Duck with Grapes and Cassis Sauce

There are few dishes more suited to a grand occasion, especially in the cooler weather, than a fine duck roasted and served with a richly flavoured sweet sauce that has a fruity addition such as grapes, cherries or pears.

1 DUCKLING ABOUT 2 KG (4 LBS)

A LITTLE OLIVE OIL

CELERY LEAVES

½ ONION, CHOPPED

A STRIP OF LEMON PEEL

SALT

2 TEASPOONS PLAIN (ALL-PURPOSE) FLOUR

FRESHLY GROUND PEPPER

1 LARGE GARLIC CLOVE, PEELED

250 G (8 OZ) LARGE GRAPES, PEELED

2 TABLESPOONS SHERRY OR RASPBERRY VINEGAR
   (PAGE 154)

2 TABLESPOONS CREME DE CASSIS (BLACKCURRANT
   LIQUEUR) OR PORT

Remove the neck from the duck and cut off the wing tips. Heat the oil in a small pan and brown the neck and wing tips all over. Cover with water and add a few celery leaves and the chopped onion. Half-cover and simmer gently for about 1 hour.

Wipe the duckling inside and out with a kitchen paper towel. Put some celery leaves and the lemon peel in the cavity and season all over with salt. Prick the skin of the duck all over and tie with string into a neat shape.

Place the flour and some salt and pepper in a large oven bag and shake the bag to coat the inside all over with flour. Place the duck and the garlic in the oven bag, tie up the opening and prick the bag once near the tie end. (Instead of using an oven bag, you can wrap the duck in aluminium foil.) Place on a roasting rack in a baking dish and cook in a preheated oven at 230°C (450°F) for 10 minutes, then reduce the temperature to 220°C (425°F) and continue to cook for 1 hour more.

Remove the duck from the oven bag and pour the juices into a jug. Place the duck on the roasting rack and return it to the oven for a further 10 minutes. Set the duck aside to keep warm. Place the baking dish over gentle heat and lightly sauté the grapes in a little of the duck fat (taken from the juices in the jug), just for a minute, until heated. Remove the grapes with a slotted spoon and set aside. Pour in the sherry or vinegar and crème de cassis, reduce the liquid by half over a high heat, then add the strained duck stock (made from the neck and wing tips) and the reserved jug juices from the bag which have been skimmed of fat. Reduce over a moderate heat until a syrupy sauce has been formed, then add the grapes.

Place the duck whole on a warmed serving dish or carve the breast into thin slices and cut off the leg and wing joints with a little of the breast meat. Spoon a little of the sauce over the duck and scatter with the grapes. Serve the remaining sauce separately.

SERVES 4

Roast Duck with Grapes and Cassis Sauce is a lovely autumn dish. Cassis is a blackcurrant liqueur from France.

French-roasted Chicken with Pears

1 CHICKEN ABOUT 1.8 KG (4 LBS), NECK REMOVED
125 G (4 OZ) BUTTER
1 TEASPOON DRIED TARRAGON
SALT AND FRESHLY GROUND PEPPER
2 CUPS (16 FL OZ) FRUITY WHITE WINE
1 TABLESPOON BUTTER
3 FIRM, RIPE PEARS, HALVED AND CORED
3 EGG YOLKS
FRESH TARRAGON OR OTHER GREEN, TO GARNISH

Wipe the chicken inside and out with kitchen paper towels. Put 15 g (½ oz) of butter and the tarragon, salt and pepper inside the chicken, then tie the legs together. Rub 30 g (1 oz) of butter over the skin of the chicken. Place in a baking dish with ½ cup (4 fl oz) of the wine.

Cover with a piece of buttered baking paper (parchment) and roast in a preheated oven at 190°C (375°F) for 1¼ hours. Baste occasionally with the juices and turn the chicken 3 times.

Meanwhile, heat the tablespoon of butter in a saucepan and sauté the pear halves until lightly coloured. Add the remaining wine and poach gently until the pears are tender, without breaking. Remove the pears carefully with a slotted spoon, place in a dish and cover with foil to keep warm.

When the chicken is cooked, skim the fat off the pan juices, then pour the juices into the wine poaching liquid. Boil over a high heat until the liquid is reduced to about ¾ cup (7 fl oz). Whisk the remaining butter into the liquid in small pieces. Beat the egg yolks, stir in a little of the hot liquid, then whisk this back into the hot sauce. Stir over a very gentle heat until thickened slightly, without boiling. Season to taste with salt and pepper.

Place the chicken, whole or cut into serving pieces, on a heated platter. Arrange the pear halves around it and coat them with the sauce. Garnish with fresh tarragon. Reserve a little sauce to offer in a sauceboat.

SERVES 6

Quail in Grape Leaves

Serve this dish in a rustic fashion without the grape garnish and sauce; this way, fingers are quite in order and there should be plenty of crusty bread to mop up the juices. Or in a more formal way with the pancetta and vine leaves removed; the peeled muscat grapes and clear brown sauce are used to finish the quail.

6 QUAIL
12 PREPARED GRAPE LEAVES (CANNED OR FRESH, THE LATTER BLANCHED)
6 SLICES OF PANCETTA (ITALIAN CURED HAM) OR BACON RASHERS (SLICES)
60 G (2 OZ) BUTTER, MELTED
SALT AND FRESHLY GROUND PEPPER
225 G (7 OZ) MUSCAT OR SMALL CURRANT GRAPES
1 TABLESPOON COGNAC
1 CUP (8 FL OZ) GOOD BROWN STOCK OR CANNED CONSOMMÉ
1 TABLESPOON ORANGE LIQUEUR
15 G (½ OZ) BUTTER, CUT INTO SMALL PIECES

Wipe the quail and cover the breasts with blanched grape leaves. Wrap a slice of pancetta around each and secure it with a toothpick (cocktail stick). Place the quail in a roasting pan with the melted butter and cook in a preheated oven at 200°C (400°F) for 7–10 minutes on each side, basting every now and then, until they are tender. Transfer to a serving dish. The pancetta and the vine leaf can be left intact or removed. Season the quail with salt and pepper.

Return the quail to the pan, breast side up, and surround them with the grapes. Roast for a few minutes. Transfer the quail and grapes to a platter and keep warm while making the sauce.

Deglaze the baking dish with the cognac, scraping up the brown bits clinging to the bottom, and add the stock and orange liqueur. Bring the liquid to the boil over a high heat and season with salt and pepper. Reduce the heat and whisk in the pieces of butter until the sauce has thickened slightly. Pour the sauce over the quail and grapes.

SERVES 3–4

Persian Chicken with Peaches

6–8 CHICKEN PIECES (BREAST HALVES, THIGHS, DRUMSTICKS)
1 TEASPOON CHILLI POWDER
1 TEASPOON GROUND CINNAMON
½ TEASPOON EACH GROUND CUMIN AND GROUND TURMERIC
SALT
90 G (3 OZ) BUTTER
4 CUPS (1¾ IMP. PT) WATER
1 LARGE ONION, THINLY SLICED
2 CUPS (10 OZ) LONG-GRAIN RICE, WELL WASHED
½ TEASPOON SAFFRON THREADS SOAKED IN 1 TABLESPOON BOILING WATER (OPTIONAL)
½ CUP (3 OZ) RAISINS
3 PEACHES, PEELED AND SLICED
60 G (2 OZ) BUTTER, MELTED

Remove any fat from the chicken pieces and trim excess bones such as backbone and rib bones. Combine the spices and rub over the chicken. Heat 30 g (1 oz) of the butter in a large frying pan (skillet) and gently sauté the sliced onion until soft and golden. Remove and set aside. Add a little more butter to the pan and sauté the chicken pieces on both sides until golden.

Bring the water to the boil and add the rice. Bring back to the boil, reduce the heat and cook, partially covered, for about 15 minutes. Drain and rinse with more water for a few minutes.

Melt 60 g (2 oz) of the butter in a heavy pan and add the saffron water, if using. Add the rice and fork it through. Put half the rice mixture in a flameproof casserole, arrange the chicken pieces on top and scatter over the raisins, sliced peaches and fried onion.

Top with the remaining rice and over it pour the melted butter. Cover tightly and simmer over a gentle heat, without stirring, for about 30 minutes until the chicken and rice are very tender.

SERVES 4–6

Chicken Breasts with Mango Salsa

This is a lovely summer dish—the cooking is easy and the mango is in season. Fresh peaches, nectarines or plums can replace the mango.

4 TABLESPOONS FRESH LIME JUICE
1 TABLESPOON GRATED GINGER
2 GARLIC CLOVES, ROUGHLY CHOPPED
1 TEASPOON CAYENNE PEPPER
6 CHICKEN BREAST HALVES, SKINNED AND BONED
MANGO SALSA
1 RIPE MANGO, PEELED, SEEDED AND DICED
1 SMALL RED ONION, CHOPPED
3 TABLESPOONS CHOPPED FRESH CORIANDER
3 TABLESPOONS LIME OR LEMON JUICE
1 TABLESPOON CHOPPED FRESH MINT
1 TABLESPOON LIGHT OLIVE OIL
1 SMALL RED CHILLI (CHILI PEPPER), SEEDED AND FINELY CHOPPED
FRESHLY GROUND PEPPER

1 TABLESPOON LIGHT OLIVE OIL
8 THIN LIME OR LEMON SLICES
CORIANDER (CHINESE PARSLEY) SPRIGS, TO GARNISH

In a wide, shallow bowl, mix together the lime juice, ginger, garlic and cayenne. Add the prepared chicken breast halves, turn to coat all over with the marinade and leave for several hours to marinate.

Mango Salsa. Combine the salsa ingredients in a mixing bowl. Cover and leave in the refrigerator until ready to serve.

Heat the oil in a sauté pan and sauté the chicken over a moderately high heat until browned, about 4 minutes on each side. Transfer to a platter and keep warm. Add the lime or lemon slices to the pan and sauté until coloured on both sides. Arrange two on each serving plate with a chicken breast half and place a spoonful of Mango Salsa next to the chicken. Garnish with sprigs of coriander.

SERVES 4

SWEET BITES

Delicious pastes of ground almonds and sugar, coloured and fashioned into fanciful shapes; brilliant orange cumquats, brandied or glacéed (candied); rich and dark chocolate truffles or fudge; the crystal clear and rosy pink Turkish delight—these are foods of the gods. It's when cooking confectionery and sweet treats that can be eaten with just one bite that magic and fantasy enter the kitchen. We are not cooking for sustenance now, rather to please our whimsical fancy.

Nougat

I like to add glacé (candied) cherries to nougat even though the part around the cherries tends to soften. You might find the nougat will be different each time you make it, sometimes softer and other times firmer. It all depends on how much you beat it and how accurately you gauge the temperature. A good electric mixer is essential, one with a strong motor that can stand the weight of the mixture. Rice paper is another essential, available from specialist food stores.

2 CUPS (1 LB) SUGAR

1 CUP (8 FL OZ) GLUCOSE

½ CUP (4 FL OZ) HONEY

3 TABLESPOONS WATER

2 EGG WHITES

1 CUP (5 OZ) EACH TOASTED HAZELNUTS AND
    ALMONDS

VANILLA ESSENCE (EXTRACT), ROSE-WATER OR
    ORANGE FLOWER WATER

60 G (2 OZ) BUTTER, SOFTENED

4 TABLESPOONS GLACÉ (CANDIED) CHERRIES,
    HALVED (OPTIONAL)

In a heavy pan, heat the sugar with the glucose, honey and water. When melted, increase the heat and cook the syrup until it reaches the 'hard ball' temperature of 130°C (266°F) or firm shapes form when a little of the mixture is dropped in cold water.

Meanwhile, have ready the egg whites, beaten until stiff, in the bowl of an electric mixer. With the motor running, add half the syrup in a slow, steady stream, then return the syrup to the heat, still beating the egg white and syrup mixture.

Cook the remaining syrup until it reaches the 'crack' temperature of 154°C (310°F), when a little of the mixture dropped in cold water forms threads that are brittle, then slowly pour this into the egg-white mixture, still with the motor running. Continue beating until the mixture is very thick, all the time keeping your eye on the motor of the mixer to check it is not overheating.

Quickly add the nuts, flavouring and butter, mixing thoroughly. At this stage, add the glacé cherries, if liked. Have ready a 28 x 20 x 3 cm (11 x 8 x 1½ in) pan lined with rice paper and pour in the nougat mixture. Top the mixture with more rice paper, using the palm of your hand to smooth the surface.

Leave to cool and set before cutting into small rectangles with a hot wet knife (keep the knife in a jug of hot water on the work bench). Wrap each piece in a square of cellophane and store.

Fresh Dates Stuffed with Cream Cheese

At any party, dates stuffed with cheese are usually one of the successes of the evening, a bonus for those who appreciate a touch of sweetness in their pre-dinner savouries.

125 G (4 OZ) CREAM CHEESE SUCH AS NEUFCHÂTEL

1 TABLESPOON GRATED ORANGE PEEL

1 TEASPOON ORANGE-FLAVOURED LIQUEUR

ABOUT 20 FRESH DATES

Cream the cheese and blend in the orange peel and liqueur. Slit the top of each date, remove the pit, and spoon a little of the flavoured cream cheese across the slit.

Overleaf: Dark and rich Panforte, the fabulous sweet cake from Siena in Italy, on the right; and Nougat, a sweetmeat made with beaten egg white, roasted nuts and honey.

Quince Cheese

A delicious sweetmeat to serve with coffee or as an addition to a cheese board, especially with fresh soft cheeses. For sweetmeats, roll squares or oblong shapes in caster (superfine) sugar. For the cheese board, the quince cheese looks best served in a wedge for people to cut off pieces as they wish.

6 QUINCES
SUGAR TO MEASURE

Rub the quinces with a cloth to remove the down. Bake whole and unpeeled in a baking dish (roasting pan) in a preheated oven at 180°C (350°F) until tender. This may take up to 3 hours. Alternatively, quarter the quinces without peeling and cook them in a heavy, covered saucepan with ½ cup (4 fl oz) of water until tender and a good deep pink colour.

Once cooked, allow the quinces to cool and slice them, still without peeling, into a bowl, discarding cores, seeds and any bruised or hard bits. Put the quinces though a mouli sieve or rub them through an ordinary sieve.

Weigh the purée and place it in a large heavy saucepan with an equal weight of sugar. Heat gently until the sugar dissolves, then boil, stirring frequently, until the mixture begins to candy and comes away from the sides and base of the pan. Take great care with the boiling paste, as it can erupt and spit. The paste will turn a wonderful shade of deep, glowing rusty orange.

Remove from the heat and leave to cool for a few minutes before putting into round or rectangular cake pans. Spread the mixture to an even 2 cm (¾ in) depth and leave in the oven at 120°C (250°F) for 4–5 hours to dry out. Cool and cut into large wedges or slabs, wrapping each one in aluminium foil. Store in a cool, dry spot. Well-stored, the quince cheese will keep for months.

Mixed spice is made up of 4 parts cinnamon, 2 parts ground ginger, 1 part ground nutmeg and 1 part ground cloves.

Panforte

Devotees of panforte, the traditional nut and fruit cake of Siena, Italy, say this recipe makes the real thing. It is rich and spicy as it should be. Small, individual cakes make wonderful Christmas gifts.

1½ CUPS (8 OZ) EACH BLANCHED ALMONDS AND
    HAZELNUTS
1¼ CUPS (10 OZ) SUGAR
¾ CUP (10 OZ) HONEY
2 CUPS (8 OZ) PLAIN (ALL-PURPOSE) FLOUR
1 TABLESPOON GROUND CINNAMON
1 TEASPOON MIXED SPICE
750 G (1½ LBS) DRIED FRUITS, USING A MIXTURE OF
    CURRANTS, RAISINS, AND MIXED PEEL
ICING (CONFECTIONERS') SUGAR, FOR DUSTING

Lay the almonds and hazelnuts on a baking tray (sheet) and roast in the oven at 180°C (350°F) until golden. In a heavy saucepan, melt the sugar and honey together over a gentle heat, then allow to boil until it reaches a temperature of 116°C (240°F) on a sugar thermometer or, when a little of the mixture is dropped in cold water does not disintegrate, but flattens of its own accord when picked up with the fingers.

Meanwhile, sift the flour and spices into a bowl. Add the toasted nuts and the fruit. When the syrup has reached the required temperature, pour it into the bowl. Mix all the ingredients quickly and thoroughly together. Tip into two 25 cm (10 in) cake pans —or one pan 28 x 38 x 2.5 cm (11 x 15 x 1 in) or a little larger—which have been lined with baking paper (parchment). Pat the batter into the pans with hands that have been dipped in water.

Bake in the preheated oven at 160°C (325°F) for 45 minutes. Cool and store liberally dusted with icing sugar and wrapped airtight. Cut into wedges or rectangles to serve. The flavours develop and improve with age.

MAKES 2 CAKES

Marzipan

A European Christmas wouldn't be the same without marzipan sweetmeats, often moulded into little fruits and vegetables, pink pigs and other animals to ornament the Christmas tree. Simpler sweets can be made by moulding delicately coloured marzipan between walnut halves or pressing it into a plump prune and coating it in fine sugar. Placed in tiny paper cups and arranged in neat rows in a small box, these little sweetmeats make a very special gift. If you'd like to make your own marzipan, here is the recipe. A very suitable alternative is the excellent Danish commercial brand, Odense, available in rolls.

2 CUPS (1 LB) SUGAR
¾ CUP (6 FL OZ) WATER
3 CUPS (12 OZ) GROUND ALMONDS
2 EGG WHITES
1 TEASPOON SHERRY
4 TABLESPOONS ICING (CONFECTIONERS') SUGAR,
  SIFTED

Dissolve the sugar in the water in a large saucepan over gentle heat and boil steadily without stirring for 10 minutes, or until the mixture forms a 'soft ball' when a little is dropped into cold water. Remove from the heat and beat with a wooden spoon until the mixture looks slightly cloudy. Stir in the ground almonds.

Whisk the egg whites in a bowl with a fork until just frothy, add to the pan and cook the mixture over a very gentle heat for 1–2 minutes. Add the sherry and turn the mixture onto a board dusted with a little of the icing sugar.

Once the mixture has cooled a little, knead it until it is quite smooth, working in the remaining icing sugar as you go. While still warm, divide into two portions. Colour and flavour as desired.

Marzipan can be shaped in numerous ways. It can also be coloured and used to stuff fresh dates or prunes, or just studded with nuts to make a lovely simple sweetmeat.

To Flavour and Colour. Flavour one portion with sherry or rum, colouring it pale green. To the second portion add rum or brandy and pink colouring. Knead the flavouring and colouring into the marzipan until they are completely distributed. Add the colour sparingly, a few drops at a time; a little more can always be added if the colour is not distinct. At this stage, the marzipan may be wrapped in waxed paper or aluminium foil and stored in the refrigerator.

Marzipan Walnuts

Roll small pieces of marzipan, natural coloured or tinted, into balls about the size of a small walnut. Press a perfect walnut half into each side and roll in caster (superfine) sugar. Place in paper cups and store in a box in the refrigerator if the weather is warm. Wooden chocolate boxes are ideal for this purpose.

Marzipan Prunes

Remove the stones (pits) from dessert prunes by making a slit along one side, not right through, and lifting out the stone with the point of a knife. Roll some marzipan into a coil about 1 cm (½ in) thick and cut off even-sized pieces. Shape these into ovals, press a blanched almond or a piece of glacé (candied) ginger in the middle of each and then insert it into a prune.

Roll in caster (superfine) sugar or dip into a syrup made with 1 cup (8 oz) sugar and 4 tablespoons water cooked to the 'hard ball' stage—130°C (266°F) when tested with a sugar thermometer, or until a little of the mixture can be rolled into a ball when dropped into cold water. Place in small paper cups and store.

Alternatively, the prunes can be filled with a quince or apricot paste which has been rolled into fat nuggets and slipped into the cavity. Make two or three light indentations across the filling at a slant for decoration.

Marzipan Fruits and Vegetables

Marzipan may be shaped into tiny fruits and vegetables, which are useful to have on hand for offering with a sweet drink or coffee. They make a charming gift when boxed or presented in a pretty dish. As a cake decoration, they can add a touch of whimsy.

Marzipan shapes may be coloured either by painting the shape with diluted vegetable colouring, using a small paintbrush, or by working the desired colour into pieces of marzipan before moulding. Here are a few ideas. Once you make them, you will be able to create your own fruits and vegetables. Use the real fruit or vegetable as a guide.

Strawberries. Break off small pieces of marzipan, roll each one into a ball and then into a strawberry shape. Colour a pretty pink. Roll the shape gently on a fine wire sieve, then roll it in fine caster (superfine) sugar. Make a small coin-size hull, cut the edges, and use a little egg white to secure it on the strawberry. Colour it green. The marzipan may be tinted before moulding. Set the strawberries in small confectionery paper cups.

Bananas. Break off small pieces of marzipan, roll them into small elongated shapes, tapering at one end. Paint them yellow with small brown splashes. Set in small paper cups.

Peaches. Break off small pieces of marzipan and roll each one into a ball. Using a toothpick or cocktail stick, press an indentation down one side of each ball. Paint a peachy yellow with a brush and roll in icing (confectioners') sugar to give the peach a 'bloom'. Set in small paper cups.

Carrots. Break off small pieces of marzipan and roll them into carrot shapes. Using a toothpick or cocktail stick, press small creases in each carrot shape. Make a few green stalks and poke them into an indentation on the thick top end of the carrot. Tint the finished shapes a carroty orange with a green stem, or tint the marzipan before shaping.

Potatoes. Break off small pieces of marzipan, shape them into oval potato shapes and make a few eyes with the end of a toothpick or cocktail stick. Roll in cocoa; dust off excess.

Marzipan Figures

An example of the fun you can have with marzipan As I was decorating a carrot cake, carrots and rabbits seemed in order. The cake is pictured on page 30.

The Rabbits. Colour the marzipan a light sable chocolate. Break off pieces and mould them into pear shapes. Using a toothpick (cocktail stick), shape the leg indentations, the forepaws, head, ears, eyes, etc. You will improve as you go. Give the rabbits clothes if you like, which can be pressed on, and creamy white cottontails.

The Spade. Mould the handle around a toothpick and shape the blade.

Robin Redbreast. Shape a robin from a small piece of marzipan, then paint.

Once you get the general idea, you will find yourself decorating cakes to suit the occasion. The carrot and rabbit cake became an Easter cake, then again a birthday cake for a fortieth birthday at which children and adults alike were entranced. A violin or guitar can be made for a music lover, a soccer ball or cricket bat for a sports lover, an open book or mortar board for a student. Over to you.

Frosted Fruits

Frosted fruits make a festive edible centrepiece for the Christmas table. Use your best piece of silver, china or glass; I use a special family heirloom, a silver fruit stand. Children love to be involved in the creation of these delicacies. Suggested fruits are whole unblemished peaches, plums, apricots, cherries, small clusters of grapes, strawberries, dates and tiny red apples. Muscatels or dried fruits also can be used.

ANY CHOICE FRESH FRUITS OR DRIED FRUITS
EGG WHITES
CASTER (SUPERFINE) SUGAR

Wash and thoroughly dry the fruit. Beat the egg white until just frothy. Have the sugar ready in a shallow, wide bowl. Brush a piece of fruit with the egg white, draining away any excess, then dip the fruit in the caster sugar. There should be a fairly thin yet even layer of caster sugar. Lightly shake off any excess sugar and place the fruit on a wire rack to dry. Continue with the remaining fruit, egg white and sugar. Arrange the frosted fruits in the centrepiece of your choice.

Prunes Stuffed with Walnuts

A simple sweet dish of Middle Eastern origin, suitable as a light dessert or sweetmeat, offered on small, pretty plates with coffee or an after-dinner drink.

500 G (1 LB) LARGE DESSERT PRUNES
FRESHLY MADE TEA OR RED OR WHITE WINE
SHELLED WALNUTS, ALLOWING ONE HALF PER PRUNE
3 TABLESPOONS SUGAR
1 TABLESPOON LEMON JUICE
1¼ CUPS (10 FL OZ) WATER
1¼ CUPS (10 FL OZ) CREAM, WHIPPED, OR DOUBLE
  CREAM

Place the prunes in a bowl and pour the strained hot tea or wine over, leaving them to soak for several hours or overnight. Drain and remove the stones (pits), replacing them with a walnut half.

Bring the sugar, lemon juice and water to the boil and simmer for a few minutes. Drop in the stuffed prunes and simmer gently until very tender, about 30 minutes. Leave to cool in the syrup and chill. Serve chilled with the syrup together with the cream.

SERVES 4–6

Glacé Cumquats

An excellent sweetmeat to offer with the cheese board or coffee at the end of a meal.

Using a fine skewer, make about eight pricks in the skin of each cumquat. Place them in a bowl with cold water to cover and 1 tablespoon of salt. Soak overnight, then drain. Put the cumquats in a saucepan with fresh cold water to cover, bring to the boil and simmer until tender, about 30 minutes. Drain the cumquats and cover them with a heavy syrup—500 g (1 lb) sugar to every 2½ cups (1 imp. pt) water.

Cook the cumquats in the syrup until clear and transparent. Put them in a bowl and leave to stand overnight. Drain the syrup into a saucepan, add 4 tablespoons sugar, bring to the boil and pour over the cumquats. Leave for 48 hours. Lastly, drain the cumquats, roll them in coarse sugar and place them on a wire rack to dry, preferably in a very slow oven.

Store in paper cases (cups) in an airtight container in a cool place. If you like, omit the final drying process and pack the cumquats and syrup into a clean jar and seal.

Chocolate Truffles can be shaped and finished in various ways to add interest to a tray of sweetmeats.

Rich Chocolate Truffles

Very rich, very moreish and very French. The coffee-chocolate mixture is shaped into small balls or nuggets to resemble the 'black diamonds' French chefs prize so highly. Once made, they should be kept in the refrigerator. The great thing about them is they can be finished in a variety of ways.

1 TABLESPOON INSTANT COFFEE POWDER
3 TABLESPOONS BOILING WATER
250 G (8 OZ) DARK (SEMI-SWEET) CHOCOLATE, BROKEN INTO PIECES
125 G (4 OZ) UNSALTED BUTTER, CUT INTO SMALL PIECES
2–3 TABLESPOONS BRANDY OR RUM
COCOA POWDER, SIFTED, FOR DUSTING

In a bowl over a pan of very gently simmering water, melt the instant coffee powder, water and chocolate, stirring minimally until the mixture is smooth. Beat the butter into the chocolate mixture gradually, a little at a time, until all the butter is thoroughly incorporated. Stir in the brandy or rum, adding enough to suit your taste, and chill for at least 3 hours or until firm enough to handle.

Break off pieces of the chilled mixture and roll them into rather rough small balls. Place them in a dish containing a generous amount of cocoa powder and shake until the truffles are thoroughly coated. Place the truffles in paper or foil cups, arrange in an airtight container and keep refrigerated.

MAKES 18

A few variations for finishing the truffles:
Roll in coarsely shredded dark or white chocolate.

Roll gently in toasted desiccated or shredded coconut.

Roll in Praline powder (page 170).

Roll in finely chopped toasted hazelnuts or almonds.

Stud with a piece of macadamia nut.

Stud with a piece of glacé (candied) ginger.

Pecan Pralines

On a visit to Louisiana I became hooked on these Southern confections.

2¾ CUPS (1 LB) LIGHT BROWN SUGAR
A GOOD PINCH OF SALT
¾ CUP (6 FL OZ) EVAPORATED MILK OR (LIGHT WHIPPING) CREAM
1 TABLESPOON BUTTER
2 CUPS (7 OZ) PECAN HALVES

Mix the sugar, salt, evaporated milk and butter in a 10-cup (4-pint) heavy saucepan. Stir over a low heat until the sugar has dissolved. Add the pecans and cook over medium heat to 'soft ball' stage—116°C (240°F) on a sugar thermometer—stirring constantly. (To test for soft ball without a thermometer, drop a small quantity of the mixture into iced water. It should form a soft ball which does not disintegrate, but flattens out when picked up with the fingers.)

Remove from the heat and leave to cool for 5 minutes. Stir rapidly until the mixture begins to thicken and coat the pecans lightly. Drop teaspoonfuls rapidly onto aluminium foil or a lightly buttered baking tray (sheet) to form patties. (If the candy becomes too stiff to handle, stir in a few drops of hot water). Leave to stand until cool and set.

Note: If liked, 2 tablespoons of sherry, bourbon or brandy may be added in place of an equal quantity of cream.

MAKES ABOUT 44

Chinese Toffee Walnuts

My friend Rebecca Hsu Hui Min introduced me to this entirely Chinese delicacy. A little salt and lots of freshly ground black pepper seem a quirky addition to nut brittle, but it gives a spicy rather than peppery taste, and leaves one's mouth feeling fresh and clean.

1 CUP (8 OZ) SUGAR
3 TABLESPOONS WATER
1 TEASPOON SALT
1 CUP (3 OZ) SHELLED WALNUTS
BLACK PEPPER IN A PEPPER MILL

Put the sugar and water in a heavy saucepan. Stir over gentle heat until the sugar has dissolved. Increase the heat until the syrup reaches the 'soft ball' stage—116°C (240°F) on a sugar thermometer (see previous recipe) —then add the salt and walnuts.

Bring the mixture to the 'crack' stage— 154°C (310°F), when a little of the mixture dropped into cold water forms brittle threads. Turn the pepper mill about 20 times over the pan. Stir every now and then. The nuts will take up the sugar until they are lightly coated and sticking together in a cluster.

Pour out onto a greased baking tray (sheet). As the mixture cools, which it does quickly, pull it apart into pieces with a couple of forks. Eat the same day.

MAKES 18–20

Making Toffee
Always use a large pan with a heavy base and oil the sides.
Use a sugar thermometer for the best results.
Do not stir unless the recipe specifies this.
Cool at even temperature and, when cooled, mark into squares with an oiled knife.

Apricotina

For these rich orange balls of sweetmeat, the dried apricots are not soaked, as they would become too soft and mushy and not roll nicely. Select richly coloured, large, soft, good-quality apricots. The sweetmeats store very well in an airtight container.

250 G (8 OZ) DRIED APRICOTS
A LITTLE WATER
1-2 TABLESPOONS ICING (CONFECTIONERS') SUGAR
SHELLED PISTACHIO HALVES
EXTRA ICING (CONFECTIONERS') SUGAR

Mince, chop finely or process in a food processor the dried apricots, adding water by the teaspoon until a firm paste forms. (Knead the water in with your hands if not using a food processor.) Add icing sugar to taste. Form into balls the size of hazelnuts. Stick a pistachio half in each and roll in the extra icing sugar. Leave to stand overnight on a rack to dry, then store.

MAKES ABOUT 25

Chocolate Marzipan Prunes

No amounts are given for this recipe. The marzipan is flavoured to taste and mixed with nuts as you like.

MARZIPAN (PAGE 131)
LIQUEUR OF CHOICE
ALMONDS OR WALNUTS, COARSLEY CHOPPED
PRUNES, PITTED
DARK (SEMI-SWEET) CHOCOLATE, MELTED

Knead into the marzipan just a little of your favourite liqueur. Knead in a few spoons of chopped nuts. Break the marzipan into small almond-size pieces and push them into the pitted prunes. Using a skewer, dip the prunes into the melted chocolate and leave them on a tray (sheet) lined with baking paper (parchment) to set hard. Pop them into small paper cases (cups) to serve.

Sugared Fruit and Walnut Balls

½ CUP (2½ OZ) DRIED APRICOTS, COARSELY CHOPPED
½ CUP (3½ OZ) PITTED PRUNES, COARSELY CHOPPED
4 TABLESPOONS RAISINS, FINELY CHOPPED
3 TABLESPOONS ORANGE-FLAVOURED LIQUEUR
1 TEASPOON GRATED ORANGE PEEL
½ CUP (1½ OZ) DESICCATED (SHREDDED) COCONUT
¾ CUP (3 OZ) FINELY CHOPPED, TOASTED WALNUTS
½–¾ CUP (4–6 OZ) SUGAR

Combine the apricots, prunes and raisins in a bowl with the liqueur and orange peel. Stir and leave to macerate for at least 1 hour, stirring occasionally, then process in a food processor until finely chopped. Return to the bowl and stir in the coconut and walnuts, mixing until the mixture holds together. Shape rounded teaspoons of the mixture into balls. Roll the balls in the sugar and store them in an airtight container, separating layers with baking paper (parchment) or waxed paper, in a cool, dry place. The sweet will keep for 2 weeks or so.

MAKES ABOUT 36

Semolina Halva

A beautiful sweetmeat from India, often decorated with pure gold foil. A perfect sweetmeat to offer after a curry meal.

½ CUP (4 OZ) SUGAR

1¼ CUPS (10 FL OZ) WATER

8 CARDAMOM PODS, BRUISED

¼ TEASPOON SAFFRON THREADS

1 TEASPOON WATER

125 G (4 OZ) GHEE OR BUTTER

¾ CUP (4 OZ) SEMOLINA

3 TABLESPOONS PISTACHIO NUTS, BLANCHED AND
   SHREDDED

¼ CUP (1 OZ) SLIVERED ALMONDS

Dissolve the sugar in 1¼ cups water with the cardamom pods and boil for 5 minutes. Remove from the heat and cool, then strain, reserving the cardamom pods.

Heat the saffron threads in a spoon over direct heat, then pound them in a small bowl with 1 teaspoon water to a paste. Stir this into the strained syrup.

Heat the ghee in a saucepan and stir in the semolina. Cook over a gentle heat until the semolina thickens and the mixture is creamy. Add the syrup and stir over a high heat until the mixture is thoroughly incorporated.

Remove the seeds from the cardamom pods and crush the seeds with a rolling pin. Stir them into the semolina mixture with the pistachios and almonds.

Spread the mixture out into a thick oblong and leave to cool completely before cutting into diamonds or squares.

MAKES ABOUT 20

Turkish Delight can be coloured pink, as shown here, or green and golden to make pretty colour contrasts. Flavour accordingly.

Turkish Delight

Turkish delight must be one of the most appealing gifts to be made in the kitchen.

2 TABLESPOONS GELATINE

3 TABLESPOONS COLD WATER

2 CUPS (1 LB) SUGAR

FOOD COLOURING

FLAVOURING SUCH AS ROSE-WATER, ORANGE
   FLOWER WATER, VANILLA ESSENCE (EXTRACT),
   OR OIL OF PEPPERMINT

PISTACHIO NUTS, SHELLED (OPTIONAL)

4 TABLESPOONS EACH ICING (CONFECTIONERS')
   SUGAR AND CORNFLOUR (CORNSTARCH), SIFTED
   TOGETHER

Sprinkle the gelatine over 3 tablespoons of cold water in a cup and leave to soak for 3 minutes. Stand the cup in hot water to dissolve the gelatine, stirring very gently.

Dissolve the sugar in 150 ml (5 fl oz) water in a heavy saucepan. Bring slowly to the boil. Boil rapidly for 10 minutes or until the syrup reaches 120°C (250°F) on a sugar thermometer or when a small amount of mixture forms a firm ball when dropped into cold water.

Add the dissolved gelatine, tint the mixture a delicate colour and add flavouring. Use pink colouring for rose-water, delicate green for oil of peppermint and delicate orange for orange flower water. Shelled pistachio nuts can be added at this point.

Rinse an 18 cm (7 in) square cake pan with cold water, pour in the mixture and allow to set overnight. When quite set, turn it out, gently easing with sugared fingers, onto paper thickly sprinkled with icing sugar and cornflour. Cut into strips with large scissors, then cut the strips across into squares. Rub all the outer surfaces with icing sugar and cornflour and leave to stand 12 hours or more before packaging.

Turkish delight can be stored between pieces of baking paper (parchment) in pretty boxes, generously dusted with icing sugar and cornflour. Redust on all sides before packaging.

MAKES ABOUT 18

Russian Fudge

Fudge is well worth making at home. This recipe is particularly good. Fresh nuts of your choice can be added with the butter.

750 G (1½ LBS) SUGAR
½ CUP (4 FL OZ) MILK
½ CUP (4 FL OZ) SWEETENED CONDENSED MILK
125 G (4 OZ) BUTTER
A PINCH OF SALT
1 TABLESPOON GOLDEN SYRUP (LIGHT TREACLE)
1 TEASPOON VANILLA ESSENCE (EXTRACT)

Put the sugar and milk into a large, heavy saucepan. Stir over a low heat until the mixture is well blended. Cover and slowly bring to the boil. Add the condensed milk, butter, salt and golden syrup. Simmer the mixture until it just reaches soft-ball stage —116°C (241°F)—stirring occasionally to prevent burning. Remove from the heat and beat rapidly until the mixture starts to become thick and creamy. Add the vanilla essence.

Pour into a buttered shallow cake pan 20 x 28 cm (8 x 11 in). Mark the squares carefully and allow to set before cutting. Store in airtight containers.

MAKES ABOUT 24

Black French Nougat

500 G (1 LB) HONEY
1 KG (2 LBS) UNBLANCHED ALMONDS
2 TEASPOONS ORANGE-FLOWER WATER
2 SHEETS RICE PAPER

Put the honey into a thick-bottomed heavy pan and bring slowly to the boil over a gentle heat, stirring all the time with a wooden spoon. When the honey has begun to boil vigorously, stir in the almonds and orange-flower water. Continue to boil, stirring frequently, until the mixture begins to darken and the almonds start to sizzle. Remove the pan from the heat and continue to stir for several minutes.

Cover the base of a well-oiled shallow cake pan 20 x 28 cm (8 x 11 in) with a sheet of rice paper, cut to fit if necessary, and pour in the nougat. Cover with the other sheet of rice paper. Leave to cool completely before turning out and cutting into small squares.

MAKES ABOUT 25

Fresh Dates Stuffed with Blue Cheese

125 G (4 OZ) GOOD-QUALITY BLUE CHEESE SUCH AS
    DANISH BLUE OR ROQUEFORT
30 G (1 OZ) UNSALTED BUTTER, SOFTENED
2 TEASPOONS BRANDY
FRESHLY GROUND BLACK PEPPER
ABOUT 20 FRESH DATES

Cream the cheese, butter, brandy and pepper together and use the mixture to stuff the dates as on page 128. This is also a good stuffing for celery cut into 5 cm (2 in) lengths.

Candied Orange Peel

These pieces of candied peel are moreish and very pretty. Use them as a garnish for a chocolate or orange cake or serve them simply as a delicious sweetmeat with coffee after a special meal.

3 MEDIUM-SIZED ORANGES
2 LEMONS, HALVED
3 CUPS (24 FL OZ) WATER
2 CUPS (1 LB) SUGAR
3 TABLESPOONS GRAND MARNIER LIQUEUR
¾ CUP (6 OZ) SUGAR, FOR DUSTING

Cut each of the oranges into eight sections from top to bottom, and cut the pulp from the peel. Using a sharp, flexible knife, cut away as much of the pith as possible from the peel, then cut the remaining peel in half crosswise to make 16 pieces of each orange.

Place the orange peel and one lemon half in a large saucepan. Add water to cover, bring to the boil and continue boiling for 15 seconds. Drain, rinse under cold water and drain again. Discard the lemon.

Repeat this process two more times, each time covering the peel with fresh water and adding another lemon half.

Combine the 3 cups water and the sugar in a saucepan and stir over a moderate heat until the sugar has dissolved. Add the peel and the remaining lemon half. Bring to the boil and simmer for 30 minutes, until the syrup is reduced by half and the peel is transparent.

Remove the pan from the heat and add the Grand Marnier. Leave the peel in the liquid, loosely covered, for about 12 hours or overnight.

Remove the peel from the syrup with tongs, and set it out on kitchen paper towels to drain. Leave to dry overnight. Roll in sugar to coat thoroughly. Store in an airtight container.

MAKES 48

Date, Walnut and Almond Halva

No cooking is needed for this simple but delicious date and nut halva from the Middle East.

500 G (1 LB) DATES, STONED (PITTED) AND FAIRLY
   FINELY CHOPPED
250 G (8 OZ) WALNUTS, COARSELY CHOPPED
250 G (8 OZ) ALMONDS, COARSELY CHOPPED
2 TABLESPOONS TOASTED SESAME SEEDS
JUICE OF ½ LEMON
4 TABLESPOONS ICING (CONFECTIONERS') SUGAR
EXTRA ICING (CONFECTIONERS') SUGAR

Mix all the ingredients except the extra icing sugar together in a large bowl. Mix and knead with a hand until thoroughly combined.

Lightly dust a board with the extra icing sugar. Roll the mixture into small balls, and dust with a little more icing sugar.

MAKES ABOUT 40

PRESERVES

The custom of serving one or two condiments with a meal to give it a decided lift is a legacy from the raj. In the Indian repertoire, there is a fascinating array of pickles and chutneys that make a meal complete. Many are as hot and spicy as the curries themselves. The British in India appreciated the virtues of pickles and preserves just as we do today. Most of us love the fabulous pickles and chutneys that do so much for cold meats and sandwiches. Even a simple cheddar cheese sandwich takes on a different meaning when generously smeared with pickle or chutney. Homemade pickles and chutneys add flavour and variety to all sorts of food. A spoonful of chutney enlivens a mayonnaise, dressing or sauce, just as it helps to transform a simple grilled chicken or lamb chop into a dish fit for any maharaja.

On the sweeter side, it is a simple matter to make a few pots of jam or marmalade to preserve the flavour of summer fruits for the winter. Where would the English be without their marmalade for toast at breakfast? Who could imagine Devonshire tea without jam for the scones, or French apple tart without its glistening apricot jam glaze?

For Best Ever

Chutneys and Pickles

For pickles, always use top-quality vegetables or fruit and vinegar. After the vegetables are salted, they are rinsed and then packed into jars and covered with spiced vinegar. Pickles may be sweet or sour.

The bruising of spices before they are tied in a muslin (cheesecloth) bag releases their natural oils, which give the chutney a better flavour.

Always stir with a clean wooden spoon kept especially for the purpose. Use an unchipped enamel pan for preference when making chutneys and pickles; otherwise use one made of stainless steel. The vinegar in these preserves draws out a poisonous substance from copper or the metal under chipped enamel.

Most chutneys call for long, slow cooking—from 2 to 4 hours, depending on the softness of the fruit. With softer fruits or vegetables, often all the ingredients are cooked together, but when firm fruit or vegetables are used, some of the cooking is carried out before the sugar is added, as sugar retards the softening process.

Roughly speaking, the amount of sugar used in a chutney is half the weight of the fruit and vegetables.

Put chutneys and pickles into warm dry jars, cover while still hot with cellophane covers or leave until cold and then pour melted paraffin wax over the top and allow to set.

Remember, all chutneys and pickles taste very spicy and sharp when they are first made. They should be 'put down' and allowed to mellow for at least a few weeks or even months.

Marmalade

Make sure the pan in which you intend to cook marmalade is large enough to allow the marmalade to boil rapidly without boiling over. It should also be heavy, to prevent the marmalade from catching on the bottom.

For thick, bitter marmalade, leave all the white pith on the oranges. If less bitter marmalade is preferred, cut off some of the heavy pith before slicing the fruit.

Simmer the fruit over a gentle heat, half-covered until tender, with a muslin bag containing pips and cores. If the fruit is not tender before the sugar is added, the marmalade will not set well, the peel will be tough and the colour poor.

Always warm the sugar before adding it to the fruit; this is to prevent the temperature from being lowered too much and slowing the process of bringing the fruit back to the boil.

When sugar is added, stir with a wooden spoon until dissolved and then let the marmalade boil hard without stirring until setting point is reached.

Be careful not to overcook marmalade. This will make it very dark and cause it to lose its lovely, clear red-gold colour.

Jams, Jellies and Conserves

Use dry, barely ripe fruit in good condition.

Wash and wipe fruit before using.

Skim off the frothy scum only towards the end of cooking.

Jam may be covered while very hot or quite cold. Fruits that are low in pectin often need commercially prepared pectin or the pectin of barely ripe apples. Pectin occurs in the skin, core and seeds of many fruits. In citrus fruits, blackberries and apples there is plenty, but there is little in jam melon, cherries, strawberries and raspberries.

A conserve is sweeter and richer than ordinary jam; the whole fruit is preserved in a heavy syrup. Conserves used to be eaten with a spoon from small glasses, often taken as a sweetmeat with coffee, rather than spread on bread and butter.

Overleaf: From left: Date and Chilli Chutney, Beetroot Chutney, Bread and Butter Zucchini Pickles, Rhubarb and Orange Jam, Red Pepper Marmalade, Apple and Rose Geranium Jelly on top of Spiced Orange Pickle, Raspberry Vinegar and more Rhubarb and Orange Jam. The dishes in front contain, from left, Beetroot Chutney, Bread and Butter Zucchini Pickles, and Hot Red Pepper Chutney.

When is Marmalade or Jam Set?

There are several ways of telling if marmalade or jam has reached setting point:

1. Put a small spoonful of hot marmalade or hot jam on a saucer and place it in the deep-freeze. After 30 seconds, remove the saucer, run a finger through the jam and if it crinkles at the edges and stays apart, setting point has been reached.

2. After 15 minutes boiling, place a small amount of marmalade or jam in a metal spoon, cool it slightly and allow it to drop back into the marmalade pan from the side of the spoon. As the jam thickens, two large drops will form along the edge of the spoon (one on either side). When these two come together and fall in a single drop, setting stage is reached.

3. When marmalade or jam reaches a temperature of 105°C (221°F) on a sugar thermometer, setting point has been reached.

To Bottle Marmalade and Jam

Allow the marmalade or jam to stand for 15 minutes before bottling. Stir to distribute peel or pieces of fruit evenly.

Make sure the jars are dry, warm and clean.

The easiest way to fill the jars is to pour the marmalade or jam from a jug or pitcher.

Fill jars to within 5 mm (¼ in) of the top.

Wipe cellophane covers with a towel dipped in vinegar or brandy or whisky, and cover the jars while the jam is still hot. Tie down when cold.

Wipe the filled jars carefully with a cloth wrung out in very hot water before storing, while the jars are warm.

Label clearly.

Store in a cool, dry, dark place.

Brandied Cumquats

If you have a decorative cumquat tree, make some brandied cumquats. Use the brandy to flavour desserts, drinks, custards or ice cream. Eat the cumquats as a sweetmeat; they may be dipped in melted dark chocolate and set in paper cups to serve with coffee.

20 CUMQUATS
1½ CUPS (12 OZ) SUGAR
1 CINNAMON STICK
1 BOTTLE 750 ML (24 FL OZ) BRANDY

Prick the cumquats with a darning needle in several places. Place the fruit in layers, sprinkled with sugar, in a wide-mouthed jar and allow to stand overnight until the sugar has become impregnated with the oils and juice of the fruit.

Next day, add the cinnamon stick and enough brandy to fill the jar. Close the jar with a lid and allow it to rest on its side, shaking the jar gently and turning it every few days to distribute the sugar until it has completely dissolved.

Allow to lie undisturbed for at least 2 months. Strain off the liquor, which can be drunk as a liqueur or used as flavouring. The cumquats are now very strongly permeated with brandy and ready to eat. They can also be dried and stored as for Glacé Cumquats (page 134), if you like.

Brandied Peaches

PEACHES, PEELED, HALVED AND STONED (PITTED)
SUGAR
BRANDY

Prick the peaches all over with a fine, sharp needle. Make a sugar syrup with equal quantities of sugar and water and simmer the peaches in it, covered, for 5 minutes. Lift them out carefully, pack them in wide-mouthed jars and half-fill the jars with the sugar syrup.

Allow to cool and then add brandy to cover the peaches completely. Seal the jars and store in a cool, dark place for 2–3 months before using.

Spiced Prunes

Serve with roasted or pot-roasted pork or cold meats.

500 G (1 LB) DESSERT PRUNES
1½ CUPS (12 FL OZ) COLD TEA
1 CUP (8 OZ) SUGAR
2 CUPS (16 FL OZ) WHITE VINEGAR
4 WHOLE CLOVES
1 CINNAMON STICK

Put the prunes in a bowl, cover with the cold tea and soak overnight. Combine the sugar, vinegar and spices (tied in a muslin (cheese-cloth) bag) in a heavy saucepan. Bring to the boil and boil steadily for 15 minutes. Remove from the heat and discard the spice bag. Pour the prunes and tea into another saucepan and simmer for about 15 minutes or until the prunes are soft. Drain, reserving 1 cup (8 fl oz) of tea, and pack the prunes into sterilised jars. Add the reserved tea to the spiced vinegar and pour it over the prunes. Seal the jars and store in a cool, dark place. Leave for 24 hours before using.

Brandied Peaches in preparation. The peaches are first scalded and skinned, then cooled in syrup and bottled with brandy.

Dried Apricots in Cognac

500 G (1 LB) DRIED APRICOTS
1 CUP (8 FL OZ) WATER
⅔ CUP (5 OZ) SUGAR
¾ CUP (6 FL OZ) COGNAC OR BRANDY

Put the apricots in a saucepan with the water and sugar and bring them slowly to simmer-ing point. Cook gently for 5 minutes. Pour the apricots into a bowl or storage jar, add the cognac and cover tightly. Allow to stand for at least 24 hours. The flavour is improved if the fruit is allowed to steep for more than a week.

Serve chilled with a crisp dessert biscuit. A jug of thick cream may also be served with them.

Sweet and Sour Cherries

These cherries go wonderfully with cold tongue, pork, ham, and delicatessen meats. Leave the stalks on; the cherries look prettier as a garnish that way.

2 KG (4 LBS) CHERRIES
3 WHOLE CLOVES
1 PIECE OF BRUISED FRESH GINGER, 2.5 CM (1 IN)
1 CINNAMON STICK
1½ CUPS (12 OZ) SUGAR
1¾ CUPS (14 FL OZ) VINEGAR

Wash the cherries and prick them once or twice with a needle or thin skewer. Put the spices in a muslin (cheesecloth) bag. Dissolve the sugar in the vinegar in a saucepan and add the bag of spices. Simmer for 20 minutes, then pour this syrup over the cherries in a bowl. Leave to stand for 24 hours. Drain off the vinegar into a pan, reheat it and again pour it over the cherries. Leave to stand for another 24 hours.

Now reheat the vinegar with the cherries, bringing it slowly to the boil. Bottle the cherries with the vinegar, cover and seal.

Spiced Nectarine Butter

Nectarines are not unlike peaches, but with a smooth skin. They have a peach-perfumed soft flesh, white or orange-yellow, and when in season are plentiful. Preserve the exotic flavour in a fruit butter for spreading on bread, flavouring a tart or sandwiching together a sponge cake.

> 2 KG (4 LBS) RIPE NECTARINES, HALVED AND
> STONED (PITTED)
> ½ CUP (4 FL OZ) WATER
> 1 CUP (8 OZ) SUGAR
> A FEW STRIPS OF PARED LEMON RIND
> 1 CINNAMON STICK
> A PINCH OF SALT

Cut each nectarine half into three wedges. Place them in a large, heavy pan with the water. Bring to the boil and simmer, covered, for about 20 minutes until very soft. Stir the nectarines every now and then to prevent catching. Rub through a coarse sieve to make a purée.

Return the purée to the heavy pan and add the sugar, lemon rind, cinnamon and salt. Simmer the mixture, stirring occasionally, for about 45 minutes or until very thick and reduced by half. Remove the cinnamon, cool and turn into clean, sterilised jars. Cover and seal.

Dried Apricot Jam

Look for the best-quality dried apricots; they make a wonderful jam.

> 750 G (1½ LBS) DRIED APRICOTS
> 4 CUPS (1¾ IMP. PTS) WATER
> 3 CUPS (1½ LBS) SUGAR
> JUICE OF ½ LEMON
> ¾ CUP (3 OZ) SLIVERED BLANCHED ALMONDS

Soak the apricots in water to cover for several hours or overnight; drain. Place the drained apricots and the measured water in a large, heavy saucepan. Bring to the boil and simmer, partially covered, for 1 hour or until very soft. Meanwhile, place the sugar in an ovenproof pan and heat in a very slow (120°C/250°F) oven for about 10 minutes, until it is hot without burning. Add it to the apricots with the lemon juice, and stir gently until the sugar dissolves.

Add the almonds and boil rapidly, watching all the time and stirring every now and then to prevent catching, until a little spooned on a plate and cooled slightly will stay separate when a finger is run through it. Cool the jam for 5 minutes and pour into sterilised jars. Cover and seal when cold. Label and store in a cool, dark place.

Pectin is essential for a jam to set. It occurs in the skin, core and pips of many fruits. In citrus fruits, blackberries and apples there is plenty, but there is little pectin in cherries, strawberries and raspberries. Fruits that are low in pectin need commercially prepared pectin or the acid of barely ripe apples to be added for jam making.

Satsuma Plum Jam

Satsuma plums make one of the nicest jams. They should be barely ripe and in good condition. Jam made from these plums has a richness and tartness which are particularly appealing.

ABOUT 4 KG (8 LBS) SATSUMA PLUMS, BARELY RIPE
SUGAR, TO MEASURE
A FEW SCENTED GERANIUM LEAVES

Wash and wipe the fruit dry. Split the plums with a stainless steel knife, twist them to break them in half, and then remove the stones (pits). Crack a few stones, remove and reserve the kernels. Tie the remaining stones in a piece of muslin (cheesecloth).

Weigh the fruit and measure out an equal weight of sugar. Layer the fruit and half of the sugar in a large bowl and leave overnight. Next day, turn the fruit and sugar into a large, heavy saucepan, place on a gentle heat and bring slowly to the boil, stirring all the time until the sugar has dissolved. Add the muslin bag containing the plum stones and simmer until the plums are tender.

Stir in the remaining sugar, pre-warmed, and boil quickly for 20–30 minutes, stirring during the last 15 minutes to prevent scorching. Skim the surface, remove the muslin bag and add the reserved kernels. Remove the jam from the heat and allow it to cool.

Place a scented geranium leaf, if available, into the bottom of warmed, sterilised, dry jars. Fill with the slightly cooled jam, seal tightly and label. Store in a dark, cool place.

When making jam or marmalade, simmer the fruit over a gentle heat, half-covered, until tender, with the pips and core in a muslin (cheesecloth) bag. If the fruit is not tender before the sugar is added, the marmalade will not set well, the peel will be tough and the colour poor.

Rhubarb and Orange Jam

A recipe from a friend. Made in the microwave, it really is very easy and good.

1.5 KG (3 LBS) RHUBARB, WASHED, TRIMMED AND
    SLICED ACROSS FINELY
GRATED RIND AND JUICE OF 1 ORANGE
4 CUPS (2 LBS) SUGAR

Place the rhubarb in a large microwave cooking bowl with the orange rind and juice, cover and cook in the microwave oven for 16–20 minutes on High, until very soft. Add the sugar, remove the cover and continue to cook on High for 20 minutes, until a little of the jam jells when tested on a cold saucer.

Cool slightly, ladle into small, hot, sterilised jars and seal. Label and store in a cool place.

Strawberry Jam /microwave

Strawberries contain little pectin and require lemon juice to help set for jam. This jam is cooked in the microwave oven—a practical method when making a small quantity such as this.

2 PUNNETS (500 G/1 LB) STRAWBERRIES, FRESH OR
    FROZEN
3 TABLESPOONS LEMON JUICE
1½ CUPS (12 OZ) SUGAR

Wash and hull fresh strawberries. Place the fruit in a large microwave cooking bowl with the lemon juice. If frozen, cook on High for 3 minutes to thaw, then cook the thawed or fresh strawberries on High for 3 minutes, add the sugar, stir well, and cook for a further 20 minutes on High. Stop cooking every 5 minutes or so to give a stir, ensuring that the sugar is fully dissolved. The jam is ready when a little jells after cooling slightly on a cold saucer.

Ladle into small, hot, sterilised jars and seal. Label and store in a cool, dark place.

Apple and Rose Geranium Jelly

Tart apples make a good jelly. I try to get Gravensteins, which are the first of the new season's apples; their flesh is sweet and sour and aromatic. A friend with a crab apple tree offers me a basket of this lovely fruit each season which I use to make this superlative jelly. This is also a way of using a supply of windfall apples. If you are a keen gardener, you will most likely have a scented geranium plant; otherwise a request to a gardening friend or a visit to a nursery may be called for. This jelly is good served with roast pork, duck or ham; it is also used as a jam.

APPLES OR CRAB APPLES
WATER, TO MEASURE
SUGAR, TO MEASURE
ROSE GERANIUM LEAVES

Do not peel or core the apples, but cut out the stem and blossom ends and cut each apple across into slices (crab apples may be left whole). Place them in a heavy saucepan (not aluminium) and add enough water to barely cover. Bring slowly to the boil and simmer gently until the apples are very tender.

Use a jelly bag or have ready a large sieve lined with several thicknesses of muslin (cheesecloth), placed over a bowl. Turn the apples and juice into the sieve and let the juice drip for several hours or overnight into the bowl. For additional juice, return the apple pulp to the pot, adding an equal amount of water. Boil for 20 minutes and pour the pulp and juice into the sieve as before. For very clear jelly, use the first extraction only; for jelly of especially good flavour, combine the two extractions.

Now measure the juice. For each 6 cups (2½ imp. pts) of apple juice, measure out 4 cups (2 lbs) of sugar. In a large pan, bring the juice only to the boil. Add the measured sugar and cook, stirring until the sugar is dissolved. Boil rapidly until the jellying point is reached (105°C/220°F). Check this by dropping a small spoonful of jelly onto a saucer and waiting for 30 seconds. Run a finger through it and if it crinkles at the edges and stays in two separate portions, the jelly is right for bottling.

Have ready clean, sterilised glass jars with two geranium leaves in each. (Crab apple jelly is best left plain.) Pour the jelly into the jars immediately, filling them to within 5 mm (¼ in) of the top. Cover with a lid and store.

Apricot Jam

A straightforward apricot jam for when apricots are plentiful. Choose just-ripe apricots. Overripe fruit is lower in pectin. Plum jam can be made the same way; because plums are richer in pectin, the lemon juice can be omitted.

1 KG (2 LBS) FRESH APRICOTS
1½ CUPS (12 FL OZ) WATER
JUICE OF 1 LARGE LEMON
4 CUPS (2 LBS) SUGAR, WARMED GENTLY IN THE OVEN

Wipe the apricots and cut them in halves. Remove the stones (pits), reserving four of them for later use.

Put the apricots in a large, heavy saucepan with the water and lemon juice, and cook gently until soft and pulpy, about 30 minutes. Meanwhile, crack the four reserved stones with a nutcracker and remove the brown skin from the kernels—if the skin does not come off easily, put the kernels in hot water for a minute. Add them to the jam.

When the apricots are quite tender, add the warmed sugar. Simmer gently until the sugar has dissolved, then increase the temperature and boil until the setting point is reached (see page 145). Remove any scum that forms.

Take the saucepan off the heat and let the jam cool briefly. Stir to distribute the fruit, then ladle the jam into hot, sterilised jars. Seal, label and store in a cool place.

Crusty bread and butter spread with a homemade Apple and Rose Geranium Jelly.

Three-Fruit Marmalade

The best-known English marmalade, so good with morning toast.

2 LEMONS
1 ORANGE
1 GRAPEFRUIT
WATER, TO COVER
1.5 KG (3 LBS) SUGAR, WARMED

Wash and dry the fruit. Cut the lemons and orange in half from top to bottom, lay them flat side down and slice thinly. Place seeds and core in a muslin (cheesecloth) bag. With a potato peeler, peel the rind off the grapefruit, shred it and add it to the other fruit. Remove the pith from the grapefruit, cut it into small pieces and put it in the muslin bag. Cut the grapefruit flesh into thin slices and place it with the other fruit in a bowl with water to cover. Add the muslin bag, put a plate on top to keep the fruit down in the water, and leave overnight.

Next day, turn the fruit into a large, heavy saucepan and cook gently until the fruit is soft and half the liquid has evaporated— about 1½ hours. Remove the muslin bag, draining out as much liquid as possible. Measure the pulp. For each cup of pulp, add 1 cup of warm sugar. Stir until the sugar has dissolved, then bring to the boil. Boil rapidly for 20–25 minutes or until setting point is reached (see page 145).

Remove the pan from the heat and cool the marmalade for about 5 minutes, then stir to distribute the fruit evenly. Pour into warm, dry jars, cover and tie down when cool.

To test for setting point: place a small spoonful of jam on a saucer and wait 20 seconds, then run a finger through it, if it crinkles at the edges and stays in two separate portions the jam is right for bottling.

Red Pepper Marmalade

This marmalade has a beautiful colour and a true marmalade flavour.

6 ORANGES, CUT INTO THIN SLICES
6 RED CAPSICUMS (SWEET PEPPERS), HALVED AND
   THINLY SLICED
GRATED RIND AND JUICE OF 1 LEMON
SUGAR, TO MEASURE

Put the sliced oranges and the grated rind and juice of the lemon in a saucepan, barely cover the fruit with water, and simmer until the fruit is tender. Add the sliced peppers, bring to the boil and remove from heat.

Cool the fruit slightly and measure it by the cupful. For each cup of fruit, measure out ⅔ cup (5 oz) of sugar. Warm the sugar in a slow oven (about 120°C/250°F) until warmed through. Reheat the fruit and add the sugar. Stir until the sugar has dissolved and allow the mixture to come to the boil. Boil rapidly until the marmalade has reached setting point (see page 145). Remove from the heat, cool for 5 minutes, then ladle into hot, sterilised jars and seal tightly. Label and store in a cool, dark place.

There's no doubt that tart Seville oranges make the best marmalade. The streets of Seville in Spain are lined with these trees, which look like a picture when the fruit is ripe. In Spain they are left untouched by the locals, who find the fruit too bitter to eat and have no interest in making English marmalade for themselves.

Spiced Lemon Pickle

One of the best pickles, with a most tantalising taste. Good with cold meats, curries and grilled (broiled) poultry and meats. After about four weeks, the pickle will be ready to eat—soft, mellow and a beautiful colour. When limes are plentiful, use them in place of the lemons or substitute half the lemons for oranges.

1 TABLESPOON ALLSPICE BERRIES
2 TEASPOONS CARDAMOM SEEDS
1 TEASPOON CORIANDER SEEDS
1 KG (2 LBS) LEMONS
2 LARGE OR 4 SMALL GREEN CHILLIES (CHILI PEPPERS), SEEDED AND FINELY CHOPPED
60 G (2 OZ) FRESH GREEN GINGER, PEELED AND GRATED
500 G (1 LB) WHITE ONIONS, HALVED AND THINLY SLICED
2½ CUPS (1 IMP. PT) WHITE WINE VINEGAR
3 CUPS (1½ LBS) SUGAR

Tie the three spices in a piece of muslin (cheesecloth). Squeeze the lemons and slice the shells thinly. Place the lemon juice and slices and all the other ingredients except the sugar in a non-metallic bowl and leave overnight.

Next day, tip the contents of the bowl into a non-aluminium saucepan and gently simmer until the lemon slices are tender, about 1½ hours. Remove the spices, add the sugar and stir until it has dissolved. Boil briskly for 20 minutes. Spoon into hot, sterilised jars and seal well. Label and leave for at least a month before eating. This pickle keeps indefinitely. Store in a cool, dark place.

Fresh Apricot Chutney

This great chutney is particularly good with baked ham, roast or grilled (broiled) chicken, and cold meats.

1.5 KG (3 LBS) APRICOTS, HALVED AND STONED (PITTED)
750 G (1½ LBS) ONIONS
250 G (8 OZ) RAISINS
2 CUPS (12 OZ) (LIGHT) BROWN SUGAR
1 TEASPOON CHILLI POWDER
2 TEASPOONS SALT
2½ CUPS (1 IMP. PT) MALT VINEGAR
GRATED RIND AND JUICE OF 1 ORANGE
½ TEASPOON GROUND CINNAMON
1 TEASPOON GROUND TURMERIC
GRATED RIND AND JUICE OF 1 LEMON

Put the apricots in a large, heavy enamelled pan with the remaining ingredients. Simmer gently, uncovered, until soft and pulpy, for 1–1½ hours. Spoon into pots, label and seal.

Apricot and Date Chutney

500 G (1 LB) DRIED APRICOTS
1½ CUPS (8 OZ) SULTANAS (GOLDEN RAISINS)
1½ CUPS (12 FL OZ) WHITE WINE VINEGAR
¾ CUP (4 OZ) (LIGHT) BROWN SUGAR
1 CUP (5 OZ) CHOPPED DATES
125 G (4 OZ) PRESERVED STEM GINGER, CHOPPED
1 CUP (8 FL OZ) WATER
1 TABLESPOON SALT
1½ TEASPOONS MUSTARD SEEDS
½ TEASPOON CHILLI POWDER

Cover the apricots with water and leave to soak for 1 hour; drain. Place them in a saucepan with the sultanas and vinegar, bring slowly to the boil and simmer for 15 minutes.

Stir in the remaining ingredients and simmer until thickened.

Pour into hot, sterilised jars, seal and label.

Bread and Butter Zucchini Pickles

These pickles add a flavour boost to the usual cold meats and are a good relish with barbecues or hamburgers. They also make an excellent sandwich filling on their own, as the name implies.

1 KG (2 LBS) SMALL ZUCCHINI (COURGETTES), WASHED AND THINLY SLICED
4 WHITE ONIONS, PEELED AND THINLY SLICED
½ CUP (4 OZ) SALT
3 CUPS (1¼ IMP. PTS) WHITE VINEGAR
1½ CUPS (12 OZ) SUGAR
4 TEASPOONS MUSTARD SEEDS
1 TEASPOON DRY MUSTARD
2 TEASPOONS GROUND TURMERIC

Place the sliced zucchini in a bowl and add the sliced onion. Sprinkle with the salt and cover with cold water. Leave to stand for 1 hour. Drain well through a colander.

Place the remaining ingredients in a saucepan and stir over a gentle heat until the sugar has dissolved. Bring to the boil and pour over the well-drained zucchini and onion. Leave to cool completely. Transfer the pickles to glass jars; cover. The pickles can be eaten straight away or kept in the refrigerator for several months.

Raspberry Vinegar

An antidote for sore throats in Victorian times. Today it features in a variety of salads and sauces. Refreshing as a cordial (just a spoonful topped up with chilled mineral or soda water).

500 G (1 LB) RASPBERRIES
2 CUPS (16 FL OZ) WHITE WINE OR RED WINE VINEGAR
2 CUPS (1 LB) SUGAR

Crush the raspberries and place them in a ceramic or glass (not aluminium) bowl. Pour the vinegar over and leave overnight. Next day, strain the liquid into a heatproof jar and add the sugar. Stand the jar in a saucepan and add water to the saucepan until it comes halfway up the sides of the jar. Simmer for an hour, then strain the raspberry vinegar into sterilised jars. It is ready to use immediately, but becomes mellow and lovely as the months go by.

Above: Raspberry Vinegar makes a wonderful thirst-quencher with ice and soda water. Right: Use Raspberry Vinegar to enliven savoury dishes such as Pan-fried Chicken Breasts. Add a red Spanish or Italian onion which is sautéed, and finish the pan juices with a tablespoon or two of Raspberry Vinegar.

Beetroot Chutney

A good chutney with cold pickled pork or corned beef.

1 KG (2 LBS) COOKED BEETROOT (BEETS)
500 G (1 LB) ONIONS
2 CUPS (1 LB) SUGAR
1 TEASPOON ALLSPICE
5 BLACK PEPPERCORNS
1 TABLESPOON SALT
SPICED VINEGAR, TO MEASURE
½ CUP (2 OZ) PLAIN (ALL-PURPOSE) FLOUR

To cook the beetroot, cut off all but 5 cm (2 in) of the tops, place the beets in a large saucepan, cover with water and simmer until tender. Remove the skins when cool enough to handle.

Finely chop the beetroot and onion. This can be done in a food processor, preferably in several lots using an on/off motion, as the vegetables must not be reduced to a purée, just a fine chop.

Combine the beetroot and onion with the sugar, allspice, peppercorns, salt and enough spiced vinegar to cover. Bring to the boil and gently cook for about 25 minutes. Mix the flour to a smooth paste with cold water and add it to the beetroot, stirring to thicken; boil approximately 5 minutes more.

Pack into clean, hot jars when cool. Cover and label.

Mango Chutney

For curry devotees, a way of making the most of mangoes while they are plentiful. Use this to enhance chicken and lamb curries, or even a simpler dish of grilled chicken or lamb chops.

6 LARGE UNDERRIPE MANGOES OR 3 MANGOES AND
   4 GRANNY SMITH APPLES (APPLES SHOULD BE
   PEELED AND CHOPPED)
2 CUPS (16 FL OZ) MALT VINEGAR
1 CUP (8 OZ) SUGAR
1 CUP (6 OZ) FIRMLY PACKED (LIGHT) BROWN
   SUGAR
1 LARGE ONION, FINELY CHOPPED
4 GARLIC CLOVES, PEELED
½ TEASPOON CRACKED BLACK PEPPER
1 TEASPOON SALT
2 TABLESPOONS GRATED FRESH GINGER
1 TEASPOON CHILLI POWDER
1½ TEASPOONS GROUND CINNAMON
¼ TEASPOON GROUND CLOVES
1 TEASPOON GROUND ALLSPICE
1 TEASPOON MUSTARD SEEDS
½ CUP (3 OZ) SULTANAS (GOLDEN RAISINS)
½ CUP (3 OZ) CURRANTS

Peel the mangoes and cut them into thin strips. Place the fruit in a large ceramic or glass bowl with all the other ingredients. Cover and chill overnight.

Next day, turn the mixture into a stainless steel or enamelled saucepan. Bring slowly to the boil and simmer gently, stirring occasionally, for 30 minutes or until the chutney is thick and syrupy. Spoon into warm, sterilised jars and tap the jars on a solid surface to remove any air bubbles. Wipe the rims with a dampened cloth and seal the jars with their lids. Label and store in a cool, dark place.

Date and Chilli Chutney

This chutney is hot with chillies. The amount can be reduced for a milder heat. It is best to wear thin, tight rubber gloves while preparing the chillies; otherwise, work with care so as not to rub any chilli in your eyes or any cuts on the skin.

1 CUP TINY RED CHILLIES (CHILI PEPPERS)
1 CUP (6 OZ) PITTED AND CHOPPED DATES
1 LARGE COOKING APPLE, FINELY CHOPPED
2 LARGE ONIONS, FINELY CHOPPED
1 CUP (6 OZ) (LIGHT) BROWN SUGAR
VINEGAR, TO MEASURE

Cut the chillies in half, remove and discard the seeds. Chop the chilli halves finely and combine in a saucepan with the dates, apple, onion and sugar. Add enough vinegar to cover well. Bring to a simmer and cook for about 2 hours. Ladle into hot jars and seal tightly. Label and store in a cool, dark place.

Tomato Relish

Homemade tomato relish is lovely with cold meats, grilled (broiled) lamb chops or cheese, or on sandwiches.

1.5 KG (3 LBS) VERY RIPE TOMATOES, PEELED,
    SEEDED AND CHOPPED
500 G (1 LB) ONIONS, CHOPPED
2 CUPS (1 LB) SUGAR
2½ CUPS (1 IMP. PT) MALT VINEGAR
1 TABLESPOON PLAIN (ALL-PURPOSE) FLOUR
1 TABLESPOON CURRY POWDER
A PINCH OF CAYENNE PEPPER
1 TABLESPOON DRY MUSTARD
1 TABLESPOON SALT

Drain off and reserve ¾ cup (6 fl oz) of juice from the tomatoes. Put the tomatoes, onions, sugar and vinegar into a saucepan and simmer, uncovered, until the mixture is thick. Blend the remaining ingredients with the reserved tomato juice and stir in. Stir until boiling, then simmer for 5 minutes. Bottle in clean, warm jars and seal when cool, then label.

Apple or Green Tomato Chutney

1 LEMON, SEEDED AND CHOPPED
1 LARGE GARLIC CLOVE, CHOPPED
4 CRISP APPLES OR 4–5 GREEN TOMATOES, PEELED,
    SEEDED AND CHOPPED
2 RED CAPSICUMS (SWEET PEPPERS), SEEDED AND
    CHOPPED
2¼ CUPS (12 OZ) (LIGHT) BROWN SUGAR
1½ CUPS (8 OZ) SEEDED RAISINS
3 TABLESPOONS FINELY CHOPPED FRESH GINGER
1½ TEASPOONS SALT
¼ TEASPOON CAYENNE PEPPER OR 1 RED CHILLI
    (CHILI PEPPER), CHOPPED
2 CUPS (16 FL OZ) CIDER VINEGAR

Combine all the ingredients in a large stainless steel or enamelled saucepan. Bring slowly to the boil, stirring, then simmer gently until the fruit is tender. Cool slightly, then pack in clean, hot jars. Cover and label.

MAINSTAYS AND FINISHING TOUCHES

The art of cooking with a sweet touch rests on just a few techniques, a few recipes. Once you have mastered three or four pastries, the delectable custard of England, crème anglaise, or its French cousin, crème pâtissière, you are well on the way to a new world of irresistible pastries, pies, desserts and cakes.

Learn to make praline, sugar-coated fruit and flowers, flavoured sugars, a fruit glaze and fresh fruit coulis. These are the little touches that lift sweet things almost to an art form.

Know Your Pastry

The main types of pastry used in sweet tarts, gâteaux and petits fours are:

Rich Shortcrust Pastry. This is a rich, crisp pastry used for making English fruit tarts or pies such as apple, mulberry, blackberry, plum and rhubarb.

Pâte Sucrée. A sweet flan pastry. This delicate pastry is fine and crisp, and is often used for French open tarts and tartlets. It does not absorb as much moisture as shortcrust pastry.

Puff Pastry. The pastry of a thousand leaves. Puff pastry takes time to make, but it is not too difficult. Frozen, commercial puff pastry is an acceptable substitute.

Choux Pastry. A most versatile pastry which plays an enormously important role in the creation of many pastry sweets.

A Few Simple Rules

Always make sure the butter is cool and firm.

The secret of a tender tart crust is to add as little liquid as possible to the pastry. The more water used, the harder the crust and the more shrinkage.

Pastry must be worked quickly.

Rub the fat into the flour with the fingertips. The palms of the hands are warm and can soften the butter and spoil the pastry.

Mix the liquid into the dry ingredients with a metal spatula or fork to avoid overheating.

Always roll pastry away from you, using firm, deft strokes. Lift and turn the pastry round when necessary, to give an even thickness. Do not turn the pastry over at any stage.

Overleaf: Master the making of Pâte Sucrée (Sweet Flan Pastry) and the world of French tarts and tartlets is at your fingertips.

Pastry should be chilled for at least 30 minutes before it is rolled out. This allows it to relax and lose its elasticity. After rolling the pastry and lining the pans, chill again before baking, to avoid shrinkage.

To Line a Flan Tin (Pie Pan).
Transfer the rolled-out pastry from the pastry board to the tin or pan by first placing the rolling pin on top of the pastry and lifting one half over the pin; unroll it over the tin.

Avoid pulling and stretching the pastry to fit the tin (pan) or it will pull back again through cooking and become misshapen.

Trim off excess with a sharp knife.

Prick the base well with a fork to prevent the pastry bubbling.

To Bake Blind

Many recipes omit the vital step of prebaking the pastry case (pie shell). A good tart, whether it be savoury or sweet, depends on a properly cooked crust, yet so often you find a soggy pastry base. 'Baking blind' overcomes this problem completely.

To bake blind, line the pastry case with tissue or soft baking paper (parchment) and half-fill it with dried beans or rice or pastry weights. I keep dried beans in a jar just for this purpose and reuse them again and again. Bake in a preheated oven at 190°C (375°F) for about 15 minutes until the pastry is set.

Remove the paper and beans. Return the pastry case to the oven for a further 5 minutes to dry out the base or to finish cooking, depending on the recipe. If the pastry case is to be filled before returning it to the oven, allow it to cool slightly before filling and baking further.

Rich Shortcrust Pastry

This pastry is used for fruit pies and some tarts when a rich pastry is called for, particularly if the dish is to be eaten cold. It may also be used for savoury flans or pies if the sugar is omitted.

SUFFICIENT FOR A DOUBLE-CRUST PIE (SHELL AND COVER) TO FIT A 20–23 CM (8–9 IN) FLAN DISH (PIE PAN)

2 CUPS (8 OZ) PLAIN (ALL-PURPOSE) FLOUR

A PINCH OF SALT

185 G (6 OZ) UNSALTED BUTTER

1 TABLESPOON CASTER (SUPERFINE) SUGAR

1 EGG YOLK

1½ TABLESPOONS WATER

SUFFICIENT FOR A SINGLE-CRUST PIE IN A 20–23 CM (8–9 IN) FLAN DISH (PIE PAN)

1 CUP (4 OZ) PLAIN (ALL-PURPOSE) FLOUR

A PINCH OF SALT

90 G (3 OZ) UNSALTED BUTTER

2 TEASPOONS CASTER (SUPERFINE) SUGAR

1 EGG YOLK

2 TEASPOONS WATER

Sift the flour and salt into a large bowl. Cut the butter into small pieces and add to the flour. Rub the butter into the flour with fingertips until the mixture resembles breadcrumbs. Do not overdo this, as the butter will be blended more thoroughly later. Stir in the sugar.

Make a well in the centre. Mix the egg yolk with the water and combine the ingredients quickly with a knife. Press the dough together with the fingers.

Turn the dough out onto a floured board and knead it lightly until smooth. Roll it into a ball. Brush off excess flour. Wrap the dough in greaseproof (wax) paper and chill for 20–30 minutes before using.

Food Processor Alternative

Have the butter well chilled or, even better, frozen. Fit the metal double-bladed knife. Sift the flour and salt into the bowl. Cut the butter into small pieces and add to the flour. Process for 15–20 seconds, turning the motor on and off, until the mixture resembles fine breadcrumbs.

Add the sugar and egg yolk and sprinkle over the water. Process for about 20 seconds or until the pastry clings together and forms a ball. Lightly knead the mixture together to form a smooth dough. Chill and use as required.

Puff Pastry

Good puff pastry should rise to more than twice the size of the uncooked pastry. As it is difficult to make on a hot day, a cool marble slab helps.

2 CUPS (8 OZ) PLAIN (ALL-PURPOSE) FLOUR

A PINCH OF SALT

155–185 G (5–6 OZ) UNSALTED BUTTER

ABOUT ½ CUP (4 FL OZ) ICE-COLD WATER

1 TEASPOON LEMON JUICE

Sift the flour with the salt into a mixing bowl. Rub in 30 g (1 oz) of the measured butter in the usual way, then mix to a firm dough with the water and lemon juice. Knead until smooth on a lightly floured board. Wrap and chill for about 15 minutes.

Place the remaining butter between two sheets of plastic wrap (cling film) and beat it into a pliable cake about 8–9 cm (3–3½ in) square. Roll the dough into a rectangle and place the butter in the middle. Wrap the butter up in the dough; fold the dough over the butter like a parcel, then turn it over.

Roll the dough into a long oblong and fold into three layers, the bottom third folded up and the top third folded back over it. Give the dough a half-turn so the folded edge is on your left. Repeat the rolling and folding process. Wrap and chill for a further 15 minutes.

Continue rolling and folding this way until the pastry has had six turns in all. Try to keep all the edges square as you roll and fold, so that the pastry rises evenly. Chill again if necessary.

Choux Pastry

Used for cream puffs, éclairs and profiteroles, and similar light confections. The pastry is made by an unusual method. For baking choux, the oven must be very hot and the pastry not taken from the oven until it is quite firm. A well-cooked puff is golden brown and light in the hand. Once you have mastered the rules, you have at your fingertips one of the most versatile of pastries.

1 CUP (8 FL OZ) WATER
125 G (4 OZ) BUTTER
½ TEASPOON SALT
½ TEASPOON SUGAR
1 CUP (4 OZ) PLAIN (ALL-PURPOSE) FLOUR
4 EGGS, 55 G (1¾ OZ)

Put the water, butter, salt and sugar into a small saucepan and bring slowly to the boil. Sift the flour onto a piece of kitchen paper and tip the flour all at once into the boiling liquid. Beat vigorously over a low heat with a wooden spoon until the ingredients are combined and the mixture comes away from the sides of the saucepan. Do not overbeat at this stage.

Remove from the heat and turn the mixture into a bowl; spread the mixture around the bowl to help it cool. Beat in the eggs one at a time, beating well after each addition.

Shape as directed in the recipe. For small puffs or éclairs, bake at 220°C (425°F) for 12 minutes, then reduce the heat to 180°C (350°F) and bake until golden brown and light in the hand, about 12–15 minutes, depending on size.

To make these Beignets Soufflés, carefully drop teaspoons of choux pastry into hot oil and deep-fry until light golden and fluffy inside. Dredge well with granulated or icing (confectioners') sugar.

Pâte Sucrée (Sweet Flan Pastry)

This crisp, short, sweet pastry is used for open fruit tarts, flan cases (shells) and tartlets. Its success lies in careful blending of the ingredients and lightness in handling. No liquid other than egg yolks is usually added; this is why it holds its shape. The method differs from English pastry making. This recipe makes enough for a 20 cm (8 in) flan case or 12 tartlets.

1 CUP (4 OZ) PLAIN (ALL-PURPOSE) FLOUR
A PINCH OF SALT
60 G (2 OZ) UNSALTED BUTTER
4 TABLESPOONS CASTER (SUPERFINE) SUGAR
2 EGG YOLKS
2 DROPS VANILLA ESSENCE (EXTRACT)

Sift the flour with the salt onto a pastry board or marble slab and make a well in the centre. Place the remaining ingredients into the centre. Work the centre ingredients together with the fingertips of one hand. The movement of the fingertips working on these centre ingredients is rather like that of a chicken pecking corn.

Using a metal spatula, quickly draw in the flour. Knead the pastry lightly until smooth. Wrap in greaseproof (wax) paper and chill for 1 hour or more before using, and again after it has been rolled out. Prick the base of the flan case (pie shell) just before putting it in the oven. Bake in a preheated oven at 190°C (375°F) until the pastry is a pale biscuit colour.

Food Processor Alternative
Have the butter well chilled or frozen. Fit the double-bladed knife. Sift the flour and salt into the bowl. Cut the butter into small pieces and add to the bowl. Process the mixture for 15–20 seconds or until the mixture resembles fine breadcrumbs. Add the egg yolks, sugar and vanilla, and process for a further 20–30 seconds until the mixture starts to cling together. Turn out onto a floured surface and form into a ball. Knead lightly until smooth and wrap and chill before using.

Crème au Beurre (Butter Cream)

One of the smoothest, most delectable but easy-to-make creams which can be used in many recipes, including sponge-based or meringue desserts and gâteaux. Its advantage is that it is not too rich nor sickly.

½ CUP (4 OZ) SUGAR
½ CUP (4 FL OZ) WATER
5 EGG YOLKS
½ TEASPOON VANILLA ESSENCE (EXTRACT)
250 G (8 OZ) UNSALTED BUTTER, SOFTENED

Dissolve the sugar in the water over very gentle heat, then bring to the boil, boiling until the syrup falls in a thread from the spoon—if you have a sugar thermometer it should register 112°C (234°F). Beat the yolks for 1 minute, preferably using an electric beater; while still beating, add the hot syrup in a very slow stream. Continue beating until the mixture has cooled.

Add the vanilla essence and then the butter, beating it, not too vigorously, in small pieces until thoroughly incorporated and the butter cream is light and fluffy. If it seems too soft, chill it for a few minutes.

Butter cream will keep in the refrigerator for up to a week stored in an airtight container. Before using it, bring it to room temperature, then mix well until smooth.

Chocolate Butter Cream. Melt 90 g (3 oz) of dark (semi-sweet) chocolate in a double boiler or over warm water. Cool. Add this to the egg mixture after it has cooled and before adding the butter.

Praline Butter Cream. Add 3–4 tablespoons of Praline (page 170) after adding the butter.

Coffee Butter Cream. Use very strong black coffee in place of the water when making the syrup. Good freeze-dried granules can be used to make the coffee.

Coulis

Fruit coulises are mostly made with red fruits such as strawberries, raspberries or redcurrants. A fruit coulis is basically a puréed, sweetened fruit sauce and is served with meringues, tortes, gâteaux and cream desserts, even spooned over ice cream. Its tart, fresh sweetness complements such treats.

500 G (1 LB) SOFT RED BERRY FRUITS, FRESH OR
    FROZEN
½ CUP (4 OZ) SUGAR

Wash fresh fruit and purée it with the sugar in a food processor. Do not overprocess or the purée will become too frothy and lose colour. Rub through a sieve to remove the seeds.

Put frozen fruit with the sugar into a saucepan and cook until bubbling. Do not overcook or the bright colour will darken. Rub through a sieve.

Taste the coulis; if not sweet enough, add a little more sugar. Stored in a covered jar in the refrigerator, it will keep for several weeks.

MAKES 2 CUPS

Crème Patissière (Pastry Cream)

Pastry cream is used extensively in pastry and cakemaking. It is the standard filling for a fruit tart, éclairs and profiteroles. It is used to fill puff pastry sweets such as neapolitans or cream horns, and is an alternative to cream as a filling for sponge cakes. Flavouring can be added in several ways: vanilla, either by simply adding vanilla essence (extract) or by scalding a vanilla bean with the milk; chocolate, by melting some with the milk; coffee, by adding coffee essence at the end; and orange, by adding grated peel to the egg yolks when beating.

2 EGG YOLKS

3 TABLESPOONS CASTER (SUPERFINE) SUGAR

6 TEASPOONS CORNFLOUR (CORNSTARCH)

2 TABLESPOONS PLUS 1 TEASPOON PLAIN
    (ALL-PURPOSE) FLOUR

1¼ CUPS (10 FL OZ) MILK

1 EGG WHITE

½ TEASPOON VANILLA ESSENCE (EXTRACT)

Beat the egg yolks in a bowl with the sugar until well creamed. Add the sifted flours and stir them in with 2 tablespoons of the milk. Bring the remaining milk just to the boil, pour it onto the creamed mixture and stir well to blend. Return the mixture to the saucepan and stir over a gentle heat until thick, without letting it boil. Set aside.

Meanwhile whisk the egg white until soft peaks form. Stir a spoonful into the custard mixture, then fold in the rest. Continue to stir and fold, over very gentle heat, for 1–2 minutes, adding the vanilla essence at this stage. Pour into a bowl to cool before using.

MAKES ABOUT 2 CUPS

Crème Anglaise (Egg Custard Cream)

This cream is considered one of the best sauces to come out of the English kitchen. It is used in trifles; as a sauce with steamed puddings, stewed fruit and fruit compotes; and as the base for the lovely 'floating islands' or 'Oeufs à la Neige' (page 94). Crème Pralinée—Crème Anglaise mixed with Praline (page 170) is a favourite of mine.

1½ CUPS (12 FL OZ) MILK

1 VANILLA BEAN OR ½ TEASPOON VANILLA ESSENCE
    (EXTRACT)

3 EGG YOLKS

3 TABLESPOONS CASTER (SUPERFINE) SUGAR

1½ TEASPOONS CORNFLOUR (CORNSTARCH)

Put the milk in a saucepan with the vanilla bean, if using, and bring slowly to the boil. Beat the egg yolks, sugar, and cornflour together in a bowl until light in colour. Remove the vanilla bean and stir the scalded milk into the egg-yolk mixture. Stir well, return the mixture to the saucepan and heat gently until the custard almost comes to the boil, stirring continuously. On no account allow the mixture to boil.

At this stage, flavour with vanilla essence, if using. Pour the custard cream into a bowl, cover the surface with plastic wrap (cling film) and allow to cool before using.

MAKES 2 CUPS (16 FL OZ)

Meringues

Gasparini, a Swiss pastrycook from the town of Merinyghen, was expecting a visit from Napoleon when he created a confection using nuts, sugar and egg yolks. Not wanting to waste the egg whites, he whipped them together with sugar and shaped them into mounds, which he baked until crisp dry and served in saucers brimming with cream. It is said Napoleon preferred the second creation and named them after the town.

The secret of making crisp, light meringues is the timing. You must work quickly once the sugar is added or the meringue will wilt. Avoid rainy days and damp, humid weather, and most importantly, don't make them while doing other cooking. The moisture in the air will make the dried meringues weep. If the meringues absorb any moisture, they can be dried in a very slow oven (100°C/210°F) for 15 minutes or so. As soon as they are cool they should be packed in airtight tins.

Clean utensils are also essential. Fats, oils and grease, even the slightest bit of egg yolk, will most certainly reduce the volume of your meringue. Also, have the egg whites at room temperature—this maximises the air they will absorb when beaten.

Shape into shells, crusts, baskets and all manner of fancy or plain designs. These will keep for weeks, even months, in a clean, airtight jar or tin, ready at any time for a myriad of uses. Fill with cream, berries or any other soft fruits, finish with a fruit sauce or coulis, or fill or top with a piped rosette of chocolate, coffee or chestnut cream.

When I was the pastry chef at the Cordon Bleu Restaurant in London's Marylebone Lane, I kept tins of meringue in different shapes ready to make desserts, little cakes and petits fours at the drop of a hat. The customers loved them. Meringues are one of the most versatile offerings of the kitchen.

Meringues should be made in dry weather and stored in an air tight container; some cooks like to keep a copper bowl just for beating egg whites.

3 LARGE EGG WHITES
SCANT ⅛ TEASPOON CREAM OF TARTAR
1 CUP (8 OZ) CASTER (SUPERFINE) SUGAR

Preheat the oven to 120°C (250°F). Brush baking trays (sheets) lightly with oil and dust with flour. Alternatively, use baking paper (parchment) to line the trays.

Using either a freshly cleaned copper bowl with a balloon whisk or the bowl of an electric mixer, beat the egg whites, slowly at first, until frothy. Add the cream of tartar and now beat quickly by hand, or on the highest speed of the mixer, until peaks hold their shape. Gradually beat in 2 tablespoons of the sugar and continue beating for 2–3 minutes. Add the remaining sugar all at once and fold in lightly and quickly using a large metal spoon.

Pipe the mixture onto the prepared trays or shape with two spoons (see below). Bake for 1½ hours, then take them out of the oven. Ease the meringues off the trays, turn them over and make an indentation in the bottom of each by pressing gently with a finger. Then put them back in the oven on their sides for a further 20–30 minutes until they are crisp, dry and a delicate beige colour. When cool, store them in an airtight container.

The meringues are indented on the bottom so that they can be filled with whipped cream (sweetened and flavoured, if liked) and sandwiched together in pairs. The recesses hold a fair amount of cream and prevent the two halves from slipping. Pile the meringues on a glass or silver dish to serve.

Piped Meringue Shells. These may be bite-size for petits fours or egg-size for dessert. Put the meringue mixture into a forcing bag with a plain nozzle. Pipe rounds, wider at the base and spiralling to a peak.

To Shape Meringues with Spoons.
Meringues shaped with spoons can look very pretty—the ones on the plate in the foreground of the picture opposite were done this way. You will need two dessertspoons, a metal

spatula or palette knife, and a jug (pitcher) or bowl of iced water. Take up a spoonful of the meringue mixture in a wet spoon and, with a wet spatula, smooth it quickly over, piling it in the centre and pointing the two ends. With the second spoon, scoop the meringue out onto the prepared baking tray (sheet). Leave a space of at least 2 cm (1 in) between each meringue.

Meringue Fingers. Put the meringue mixture into a forcing bag and, using a plain nozzle, pipe small finger lengths onto prepared baking trays (sheets). Bake until crisp and dry, then cool on wire racks for a few minutes. Store airtight until required.

To chocolate-coat one end, have ready a small bowl with a little chocolate which has been melted gently over hot water, and a saucer of finely chopped nuts. Dip either one or both into the chocolate, then sprinkle lightly with the nuts. Return to racks to allow the chocolate to set.

Scented Sugars

A jar of caster (superfine) sugar stored with a vanilla bean is a must in the pantry for anyone who loves to bake.

Sugar can be scented in other ways, aside from vanilla. The leaves of scented geraniums for instance, which are among the most fragrant plants and worth including in the herb garden, make a lovely scented sugar. The varieties available include almond, apple, lemon, nutmeg, peppermint, and rose geranium. The flavour of these leaves is easily imparted by simply layering a handful through a jar of caster (superfine) sugar. Rose petals, violet flowers and mints will do the same. Put the leaves, flowers or petals in the container of sugar and close it tightly for a couple of weeks.

Spiced sugars also are good to have on hand. Layer caster (superfine) sugar in small jars with grated nutmeg or cinnamon. Seal and leave several weeks. Use flavoured and scented sugars to flavour cakes, biscuits (cookies), custards, creams, sorbets, ice cream or even tea.

Lemon Butter Icing

A fresh-tasting topping for simple tea breads or cakes.

60 G (2 OZ) UNSALTED BUTTER
1 TEASPOON FRESHLY GRATED LEMON RIND
1 TEASPOON VANILLA ESSENCE (EXTRACT)
1 TABLESPOON FRESH LEMON JUICE
¾–1 CUP (4–6 OZ) ICING (CONFECTIONERS') SUGAR, SIFTED

Cream the butter with the grated lemon rind, vanilla and lemon juice and gradually beat in the icing sugar until the icing is thick and smooth. Makes ¾ cup (6 fl oz), enough for 12 small cakes, 1 round or 2 bar (loaf) cakes.

Fruit Glaze

The glistening fruit tarts you find in the windows of the Continental pastry shops are totally irresistible. The soft fruits nestling in crisp, fine pastry shells are given brilliance and protection with a coat of a coloured fruit glaze. When making the glaze, choose a conserve that matches the colour of the fruit: for example, apricot for pale fruit and redcurrant for red fruits.

1 CUP (12 OZ) JAM, JELLY OR CONSERVE
3 TABLESPOONS WATER
1 TABLESPOON LEMON JUICE

Heat all the ingredients over a gentle heat, stirring until smooth. Strain through a sieve. Use warm, apply with a scrupulously clean pastry brush or spoon it over the fruit thinly. If the glaze sets too quickly, reheat it gently, adding a squeeze of lemon or a teaspoon of water if necessary.

To blanch almonds, place them in a bowl and pour over boiling water to cover. Leave them to stand for a few minutes, then lift them out of the hot water and, when cooled enough to handle, slip off the skins. Almonds bought with their skins on have a better flavour than those already blanched.

Candied Flowers

Sweet-scented flowers such as roses, violets, honeysuckle, sweet peas and scented geraniums are all edible when candied. They can be used to decorate a special dessert or cake, or add a flourishing touch to cream desserts or homemade ices. They also make an excellent sweetmeat to serve after dinner.

3 CUPS EDIBLE FLOWERS
2 CUPS (16 FL OZ) WATER
3 CUPS (1½ LBS) SUGAR

Wash the flowers carefully and quickly and gently pat dry with kitchen paper towels. Heat the water and sugar gently in a heavy saucepan. When the sugar has dissolved, increase the temperature and allow the syrup to boil rapidly until it reaches 138°C (280°F) on a sugar thermometer or small cracks form when a little syrup is dropped in cold water. Remove from the heat and allow to cool.

Place the flowers on a metal rack inside a shallow pan and pour in enough of the syrup to allow the flowers to float on the surface. Cover the pan with a cloth and leave to stand in a cool place for a few hours, then spoon over the remaining syrup so that the flowers are completely covered. Replace the cloth cover and leave the pan in a cool place for at least 12 hours.

The next day, remove the rack from the syrup and set it over a tray to drain for several hours. When the flowers have completely dried, store them in an airtight container with sheets of baking paper (parchment) between each layer to prevent them from sticking to one another.

Frosted Petals and Leaves

Sugar-coated petals and leaves can make a beautiful decoration for cakes, pastries or petits fours. They may also be offered as a whimsical sweetmeat.

1 CUP EDIBLE PETALS OR HERB LEAVES OR TINY
    FLOWERS SUCH AS VIOLETS
1 EGG WHITE
A PINCH OF SALT
CASTER (SUPERFINE) SUGAR, SCENTED OR SPICED

Wash the petals, leaves or flowers carefully and briefly. Beat the egg white with the salt just until foamy. Brush a little foamed egg white on each petal, flower or leaf using a pastry brush or a small paintbrush. Don't apply too much; just enough to moisten the surface. Shake any excess off gently.

Coat or dust the caster sugar as lightly as possible all over. Arrange the frosted plant parts gently on a tray covered with baking paper (parchment), making sure they do not touch each other. Leave to dry in the refrigerator for 1–3 days or in a slow oven with the door open for 10–15 minutes. Once dried, store in an airtight container in the refrigerator until required. They will keep for a further 3–4 days.

Praline

This is one of the best flavourings in confectionery apart from liqueurs. Slabs of toffee-covered almonds are ground into a fine powder and used for flavouring butter cream, sprinkling on ice cream or dredging over a rich custard. You can separate the almonds in toffee clusters or cut it into squares before it sets and have it as a sweetmeat. A copper sugar pan especially for making toffee and caramel is a help in cooking the praline, but not at all necessary.

4 TABLESPOONS UNBLANCHED ALMONDS
4 TABLESPOONS CASTER (SUPERFINE) SUGAR

Put the almonds and sugar in a small, heavy pan and place it on a very low heat until the sugar melts. Do not stir, but give the pan a shake every now and then to help things along. When the sugar starts to turn caramel, stir with a metal spoon and continue cooking until a good nut brown. It is important to cook it to a dark toffee (without burning) or the result will be too sweet.

Turn onto an oiled baking tray (sheet) or a heatproof plate and leave to cool and harden. Break the praline into pieces and crush it into a coarse powder using a rolling pin, blender, or food processor. Store immediately in an airtight container until needed.

Crème Pralinée. Sprinkle thickly over the Crème Anglaise (page 165) in a bowl and serve any remaining separately.

Clockwise from top: tartlet cases; Cedro, a candied citron; Candied Orange Peel; Frosted Fruits and flowers (on rack); Praline before it is ground; and Flavoured Sugars.

Index

Page numbers in italics indicate illustrations.

*Fresh seasonal fruits are the very
best of sweet things. Almost any
combination of fruit can begin or end
a meal on a high note.*